3-D PAPERCRAFT

Create Fun Paper Cutouts from Plain Paper

Pigpong: Yoko Ganaha & **Piggy Tsujioka**

DOVER PUBLICATIONS, INC.
Mineola, New York

Bibliographical Note

This Dover edition, first published in 2020, is a translated, unabridged republication of
How to Make White 3-D Paper Cutouts from Drawing Paper, which was originally designed and
published by Graphic-sha Publishing Co., Ltd., Tokyo, in 2015.

Authors: Pigpong: Yoko Ganaha and Piggy Tsujioka
Photography: Tadashi Ikeda
Production Collaboration: Hisako Rokkaku and Mitsue Kobayashi
Planning and Editing: Naoko Yamamoto (Graphic-sha Publishing Co., Ltd.)
English Layout: Shinichi Ishioka
English Translation: Erica Williams (Paper Crane Editions)
Foreign Edition Production: Kumiko Sakamoto (Graphic-sha Publishing Co., Ltd.)
This edition was coordinated by LibriSource Inc.

Library of Congress Cataloging-in-Publication Data

Names: Ganaha, Yoko, author. | Tsujioka, Piggy, author.
Title: 3-D papercraft : create fun paper cutouts from simple drawing paper / Yoko Ganaha
    and Piggy Tsujioka.
Other titles: Gāyōshi de tsukuru shiroi rittai kirigami. English | Three-dimensional
    papercraft
Description: Mineola, New York : Dover Publications, Inc., 2020. | "This Dover edition,
    first published in 2020, is a translated, unabridged republication of How to Make White
    3-D Paper Cutouts from Drawing Paper, which was originally designed and published
    by Graphic-sha Publishing Co., Ltd., Tokyo, in 2015"—Copyright page. | Translation of:
    Gāyōshi de tsukuru shiroi rittai kirigami. | Summary: "Illustrated how-to guide
    presents playful items to fashion from a simple piece of white paper: dramatic three-
    dimensional ornaments, borders, signs, wall coverings, seasonal decorations, letter and
    number chains, and more"—Provided by publisher.
Identifiers: LCCN 2019054625 | ISBN 9780486842769 (paperback) | ISBN 0486842762
    (paperback)
Subjects: LCSH: Cut-out craft. | Paper work.
Classification: LCC TT872.3 .G3613 2020 | DDC 745.5—dc23
LC record available at https://lccn.loc.gov/2019054625

Manufactured in the United States by LSC Communications
84276201
www.doverpublications.com

2 4 6 8 10 9 7 5 3 1

2020

CONTENTS

INTRODUCTION

What is 3-D Paper Cutting?

3-D paper-cutting is wall art created with paper. Paper is surprisingly strong. Here we have decorated colored surfaces, but we recommend decorating white walls too. It is fun to watch the direction of sunlight and the interaction between light and shadows.

Rooms and wall textures vary greatly. They ar inevitably affected by temperature and air. Th result depends on the environment.

In this book, we have used 80 lb. (220 gsm) pape This paper is a natural white with a fine texture.

Make It Like This

Before cutting the paper, fold it and create creases. Creases make it easy to tear the paper. While pushing the crease with your finger, create holes in the paper in the direction opposite where the fold is.

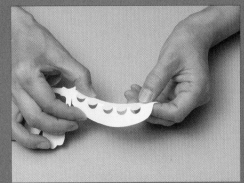

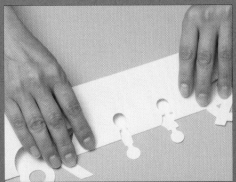

Decorative

These are decorative letters and motifs. Folding paper with a slight curve makes it three-dimensional, resembling molded plaster. This creates an antique vibe.

Crown | p. 62

Thistle p. 63

Olive Branch p. 63

Wave Borders p. 64

LOLITA

Decorative Frills p. 66

Jack-o'-lantern p. 75

Chandelier p. 68

10

Gecko, Horseshoe p. 70 Skull, Lightning p. 71 Sword, Iron Bars, Thorns, Bones p. 72 Crown 2 p. 7

Anchor, Star p. 74 Moon p. 75

A B C D E

F G H I J

K L M N O

PQRST

UVW

XYZ

Fleur-de-lis p. 80   Decorative Alphabet p. 76

Plain

These are plain lettering styles and motifs of fruit, flowers, animals, and more. Drawing paper has a fine texture, which is good for simple patterns.

Mistletoe p. 84

Peaspods p. 106

Tulip p. 81

Simple Flowers p. 82

3 Kinds of Hearts p. 81

DUCK

A B C D E

F G H I J K

L M N O P

Q R S T

U V W X
Y Z
1 2 3 4 5
6 7 8 9 0

Plain Numbers p. 89

Flowers and Leaves for Vases
p. 90
The vases pictured are glass jars.

Party Decorations p. 98

Rosette p. 99

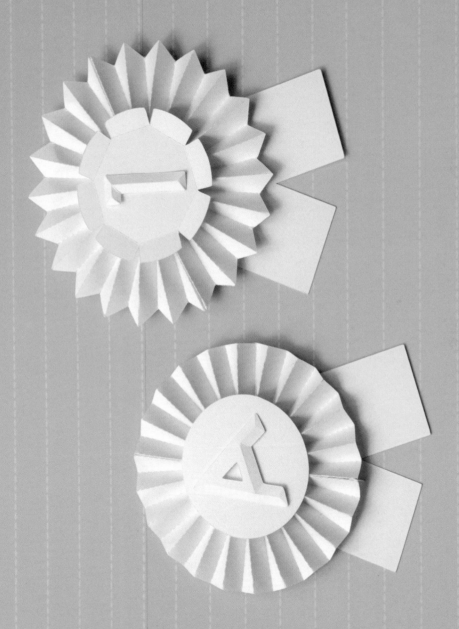

ROSE

Rose p. 102

Climbing Rose p. 102

X MAS

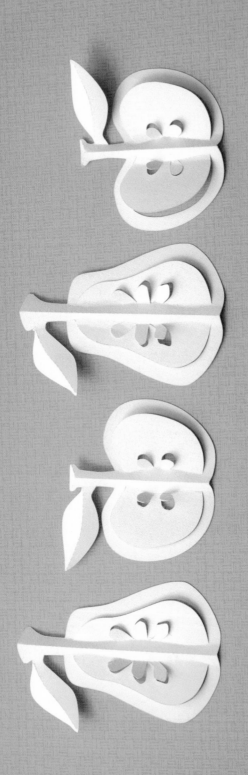

FRUIT

Apples, Pears p. 106

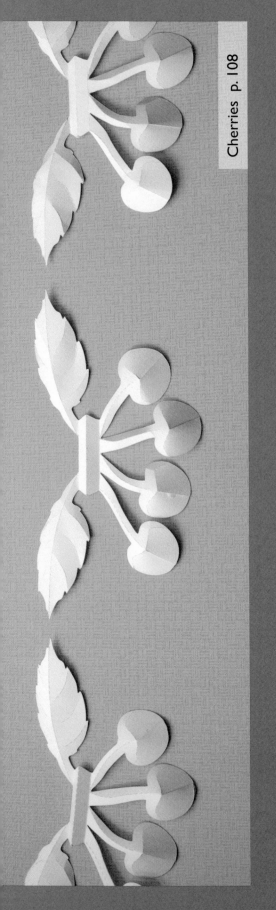

Cherries p. 108

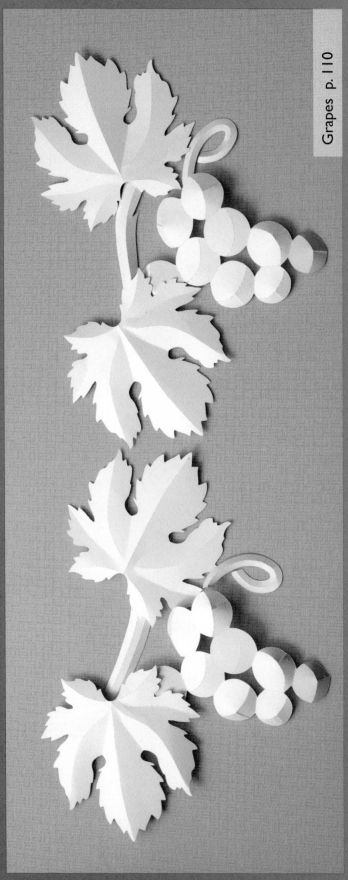

Grapes p. 110

Tags p. 112 Write a message and attach them to a present.

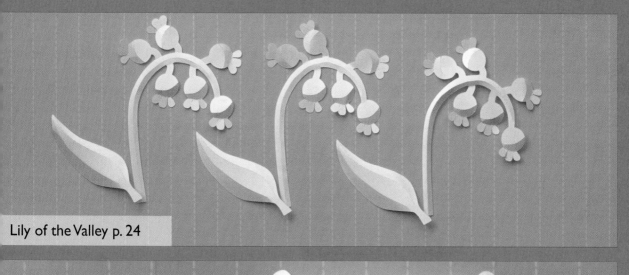

Lily of the Valley p. 24

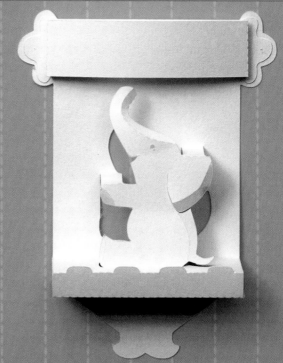

Elephant Pop-up p. 113

In this line of flowers from p. 25, the simple horizontal line that their leaves make is lovely.

Butterflies p. 114
These butterflies look as if they're flying because they're folded in half.

Mobile p. 115
The lightness of paper cutouts is perfect for mobiles.

Snowflakes p. 116
Their shape is so beautiful that we
made them bigger. These snowflakes
make a lovely ornament.

Cubic Shapes

From baskets and racks to freestanding letters and
box-shaped motifs

Houses, Trees, Fences p. 119

Box-Shaped Symbols p. 124

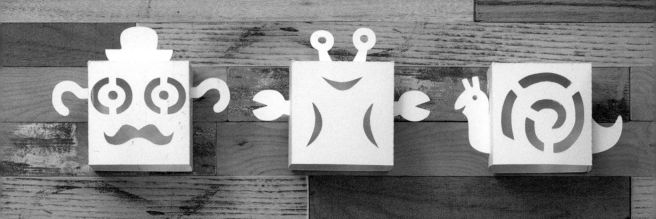

Box-Shaped People and Animals p. 121

Cubic Alphabet p. 130 Arrows p. 138

P Q R S

T U V W X

Y Z ! ?

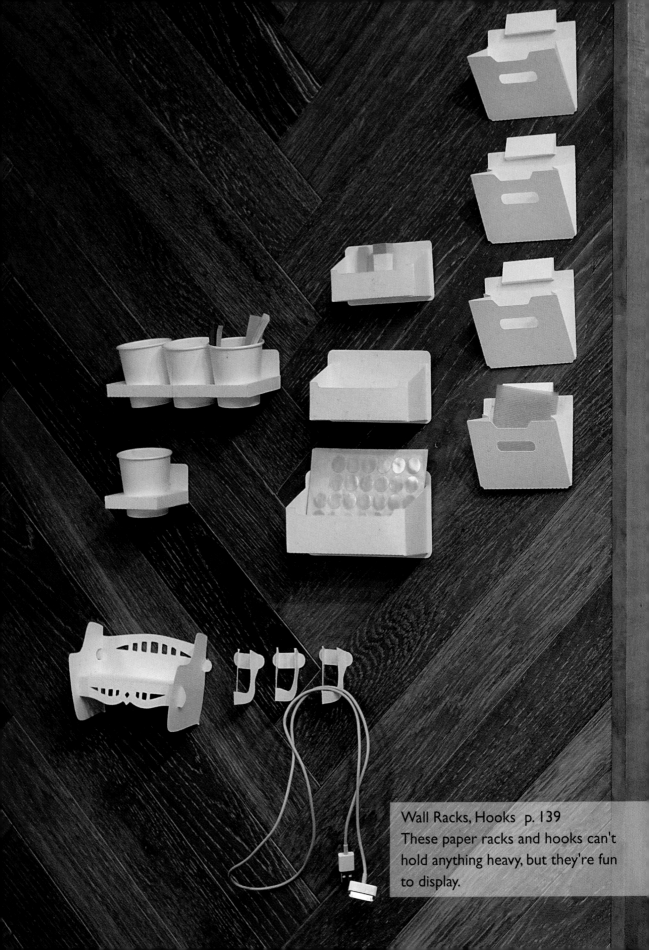

Wall Racks, Hooks p. 139
These paper racks and hooks can't hold anything heavy, but they're fun to display.

Basket p. 144
These baskets are made from folded,
overlapping pieces of paper.

Chain Patterns

Chain patterns feature letter and border motifs.
Build long, thin series of letters and patterns.

Ladles, Kitchen Tools p. 147

Decorative Borders p. 152

ABCDE

FGHIJK

LMNOP

QRSTU

Letters, Numbers p. 150

V W X Y Z

1 2 3 4 5

6 7 8 9 0

& ? ! %

Tables, Chairs, Cups, Pots, Symbols, Birds p. 158

48

HOW
TO
MAKE

These are the supplies you'll need as well as basic how-to information. With so many folds and curving lines, it might seem difficult at first. But with a little practice, you will be able to create beautiful 3-D paper art. Please read the instructions carefully.

Paper and Patterns

1 Preparing the Drawing Paper

Drawing paper is cheap and easy to find. It is suitable for cutting and folding. There are various sizes and thicknesses. Please use thick paper with a heavy weight instead of regular sketch paper. This kind of paper keeps its shape well.

Note: "Thick" drawing paper is thinner than "special thick" drawing paper.

In this book, we have used 80 lb. (220 gsm) paper. This paper is a natural white with a fine texture.

2 Copying the Pattern

When you photocopy the pattern, enlarge it according to the percentage shown on each page.

After you cut out the pattern, make creases by pressing the paper with your fingers. When you use a pen to make creases, draw the lines and dots on the reverse side of the paper.

Except for the alphabet letter chains at the end of the book, all of the lettering patterns show the reverse image of each letter.

"Special Thick"
Drawing Paper

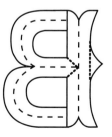

Inverted Pattern
with fold lines and
perforations included

Finished Letter

③ Cutting Out the Pattern

Cut about 3/8" (1 cm) outside the pattern.

For patterns with complicated shapes,
cut out any unnecessary parts on the inside.

④ Taping the Pattern to the Drawing Paper

Securely tape the pattern to the drawing paper with Scotch Magic Tape. Firmly attach the pattern to the paper so that it doesn't move when you're cutting the design.

It's OK if the tape goes over parts of the design. If you place tape across the cut-out areas inside the design, the pattern will stay in place more easily.

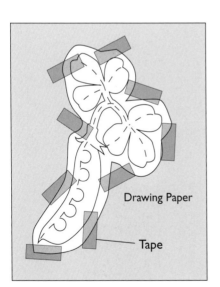

Drawing Paper

Tape

When making an inverted design, place the tape on the back side of the drawing paper.

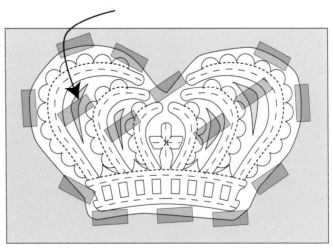

How to Fold the Creases

The dotted lines in the design indicate where to fold. Putting a perforation line in the paper first makes the cut cleaner. Even in the places with fine details, you can make perforations by pressing hard with a pen as you follow the outline of the pattern. You could cut the paper with a tracing wheel, which works best for large curves or bigger parts. Choose whichever method is easiest for you.

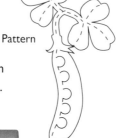

Poster Board

When using a ballpoint pen, it helps to spread the paper out over a piece of poster board.

Pattern

Finished Piece

Using a Ballpoint Pen to Make Holes

Make a dent in the paper with a ballpoint pen. For designs with many mountain folds, use the side that's opposite the finished side.

Use a ballpoint pen that has run out of ink or a pen with white ink.

Poster Board

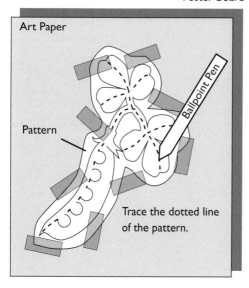

Art Paper

Pattern

Ballpoint Pen

Trace the dotted line of the pattern.

Spread the art paper out on poster board. To make the holes, press the tip of a ballpoint pen into the paper.

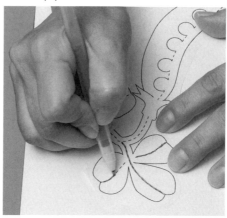

★ What to Do When the Design's Dotted Lines Look Like They Will Tear

The dotted lines on the pattern can tear when tracing the pattern, which makes the pattern slip out of place. To avoid this, reinforce the pattern with some tape.

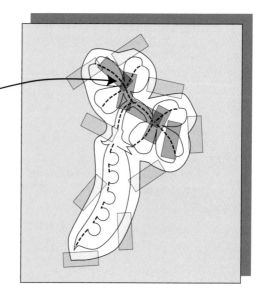

Making Holes with a Tracing Wheel

Create sharp creases in the paper by making dotted lines with a tracing wheel and then folding the paper.

Tracing Wheel
Blade Diameter: 1 1/8" (28 mm)

A tracing wheel is a tool used to cut dotted lines. It should be used with a cutting mat. Practice with scrap paper first. It is not suitable for small parts like letters and small flowers.

Without pressing too hard, follow the dotted line to make holes in the pattern. This will make folding easier. There's no need to make holes all the way through the paper.

Tracing wheels can cut very smoothly, so be careful to cut slowly. Don't use it for sharp curves or intricate parts because it can't be turned easily. For those parts, it's better to make the dotted lines with a paper knife or a ballpoint pen.

Don't put your finger too close to the blade.

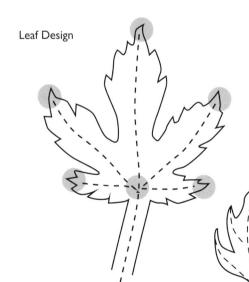

Leaf Design

The areas indicated in gray show where the perforations should stop—just before the ends and intersections of the dotted lines. If holes are cut in these places, the paper will weaken or tear. When folding these spots, make a crease with a ballpoint pen.

★ What to Do When the Design Looks Like It Will Tear

Reinforce with tape.

Thin parts, such as where the leaf meets the stem, are easy to tear. Make creases with a ballpoint pen instead of your fingers.

53

Cutting Out

Cut solid lines with a craft knife. For simple designs, scissors also work well.

Using a Craft Knife

Craft Knife

A blade with a 30-degree angle makes it easier to cut out fine details.

1 Cutting Outlines inside the Pattern

Cutting Mat

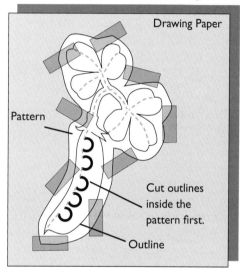

Drawing Paper

Pattern

Cut outlines inside the pattern first.

Outline

2 Cutting Outlines

If you stick tape over the cut pattern, you can continue cutting the drawing paper without tearing it.

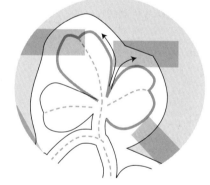

When using a craft knife, cutting outward from the center makes a cleaner cut for sharp points.

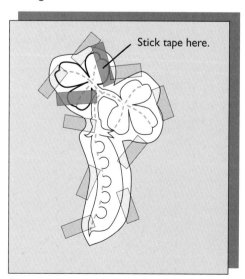

Stick tape here.

Stick tape here.

★ What to Do if the Drawing Paper Tears

Fix it with masking tape.

Scissors

Using Scissors

1 Cut Out the Outlines inside the Pattern with a Craft Knife

2 Cut Out the Pattern Outlines with Scissors

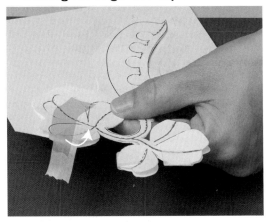

Cutting inward from the pattern outline makes a cleaner cut for sharp points.

It's easier to cut out detailed parts with sharp-pointed scissors.

★ Attach the pattern to the paper with masking tape, and continue cutting through the tape.

When cutting outlines with scissors, the pattern might separate from the drawing paper. Hold the ends together with masking tape, and continue cutting.

Masking Tape

★ Designs That Are Easy to Cut with Scissors

Designs that have only a few parts sticking out—or that have cutouts that are very close together—are easy to cut out with scissors.

It's best to use a craft knife when cutting out designs that have many detailed parts sticking out. The pattern will separate from the drawing paper easily.

Folding Paper

Good 3-D effects can be created with just a few mountain folds, even without pressing firmly or folding tightly.

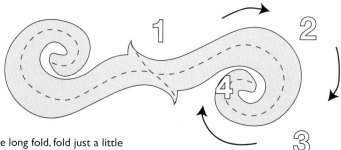

Folding Basics

Rather than making a single long fold, fold just a little bit at a time. To make a fold, place one finger on the back side of the paper under the crease, while gently pinching along the top of the fold line.

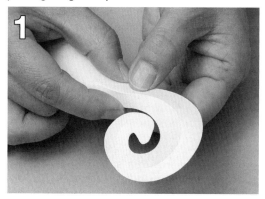

Continue folding bit by bit toward the sharp curve.

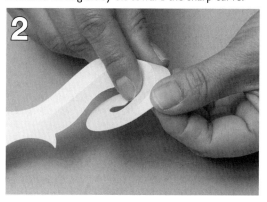

For the sharp curves, hold the paper up to see where it bends naturally and fold there.

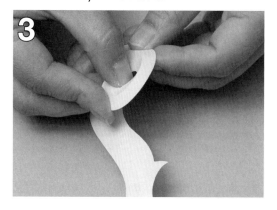

After making a slight mountain fold, pinch along the ridge to finish it with a sharper fold.

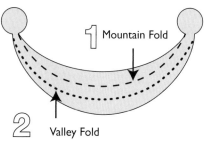

1 Mountain Fold

2 Valley Fold

For parts that have both mountain and valley folds, it's easiest to fold the mountain folds first.

Folding Plants and Flowers

Fold in this order:

Stem → Large Curves → Detailed Parts

Slide your finger along the crease while pushing up from underneath to make mountain folds in more detailed parts.

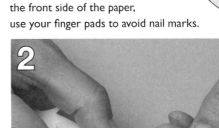

If some parts seem hard to fold, use a ballpoint pen to make another crease line on the valley fold side and then fold.

When pressing on the front side of the paper, use your finger pads to avoid nail marks.

Finished Piece

Veins on a leaf can be created by starting at the tips of the leaf and folding a mountain fold toward the center. Do not fold where the leaf veins cross.

> To make folding easier, end some creases before they reach the center.

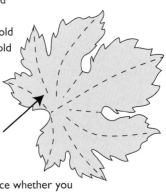

The finished leaf will look nice whether you use mountain or valley folds. Use whichever fold you prefer.

Making Intricate Folds

For parts with fine details, do not make perforations to mark the creases in the pattern because this will weaken the paper. When you've finished folding the other parts, gently push and fold the detailed parts forward with the tip of a ballpoint pen.

Folding Letters

Be careful when folding the smaller parts of letters. 3-D shapes can be made with just a few small mountain folds. Don't make the folds too sharp.

It's easier to fold if you cut a slit where the curved lines come together. This part can be left unglued.

Turn the letter over again so that the valley folds are facing downward. Using a ballpoint pen, make a dent in the concave (inward sloping) side.

For letters with mountain folds at the ends, fold the paper while pressing downward with your finger.

Slit

Cubes and Chains

Be sure to fold box-shaped designs—and designs that are connected in a chain—sharply on a tabletop. If the crease is too soft, it won't make a good cube shape.

Overlapping and Gluing

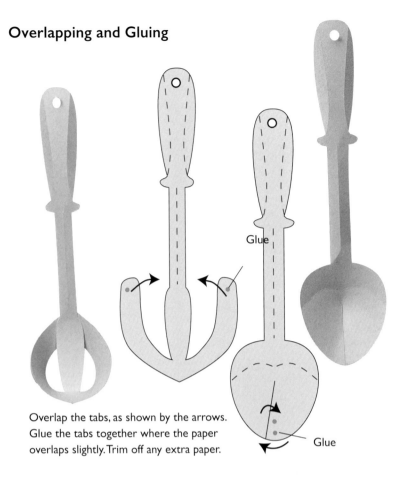

Glue

Glue

Overlap the tabs, as shown by the arrows. Glue the tabs together where the paper overlaps slightly. Trim off any extra paper.

Small round holes can be made with a hole punch.

Hole Punch

Paper Glue

Be sure to use a small amount of glue, and apply it in a dotted line. Because glue contains moisture, it can warp the paper if you use too much.

Overlap and glue the paper together in layers.

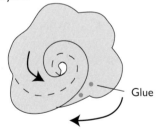

Glue

When combining two parts, hold the parts together on a flat surface and glue them together at several points where they meet.

Glue

Reinforcing

When a tracing wheel is used to make perforations in the creases, the paper may weaken or tear along the perforation line. To reinforce the paper, add a thin line of glue along the crease on the reverse side of the paper.

Displaying Your Work on the Wall

Instead of applying pressure-sensitive adhesives or double-sided tape to the whole work, simply apply an adhesive at a few points and stick your work to the wall. When choosing an adhesive, it's important to think about the material of the surface you want to decorate and whether your work can be peeled off cleanly.

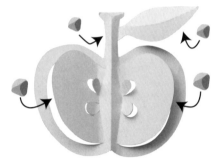

Putty-Like Adhesives

Putty-like adhesives have a chewing gum–like texture. Knead a small amount with your fingers, and stick it to the surface. One benefit of this type of adhesive is that you can shape it to fit concave parts of the design.

Double-Sided Tape

Thumb Tacks and Stapler

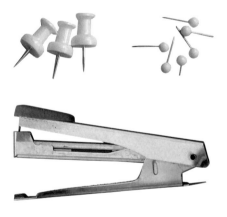

PATTERNS

To enlarge a pattern, use the percentage shown when photocopying. If you make the design smaller, it's harder to make creases and folds. The inverted patterns make it easier to perforate the pages with a ballpoint pen.

Fold Lines		
	– – – – – – – Mountain Fold	· · · · · · · · · · · · Valley Fold

Make a crease in each part. Bend the tips of the crown so that they meet in the middle, and glue them together.

Main Part

Slit

Overlap and glue together.

62

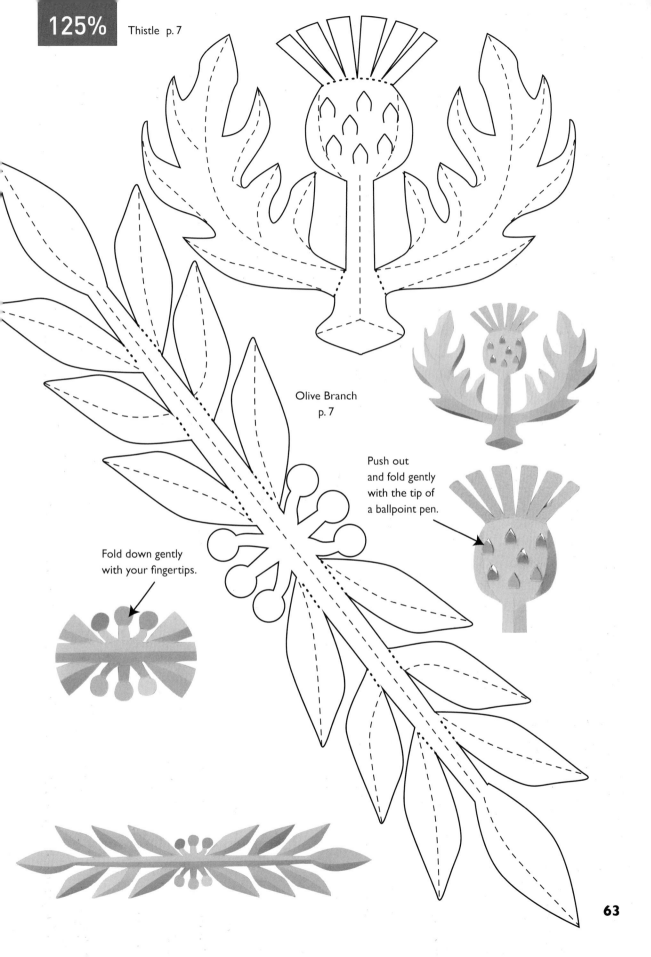

Thistle p. 7

Olive Branch
p. 7

Push out
and fold gently
with the tip of
a ballpoint pen.

Fold down gently
with your fingertips.

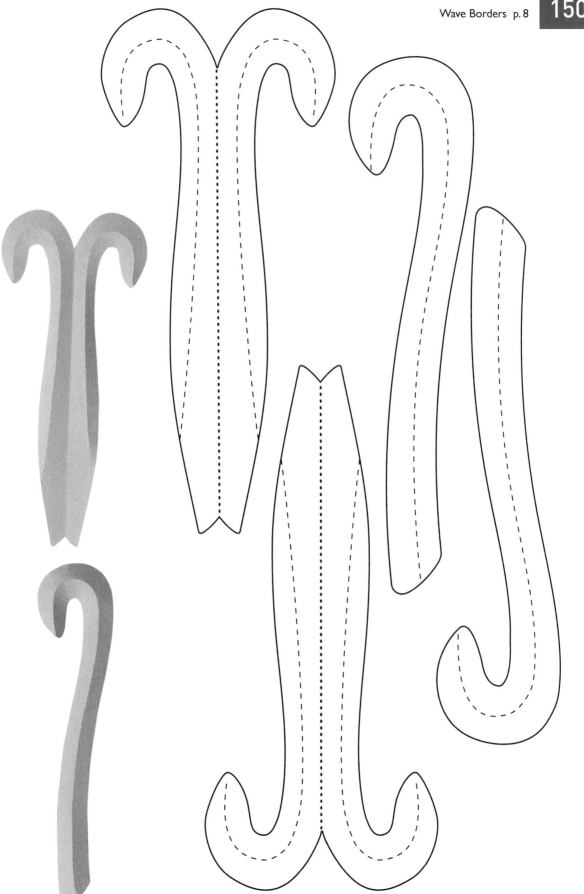

Join these parts together when attaching the finished chandelier to the wall

125%

125%

Gecko, Horseshoe p. 12

Quill Pen p. 11

Punch the holes
before folding.

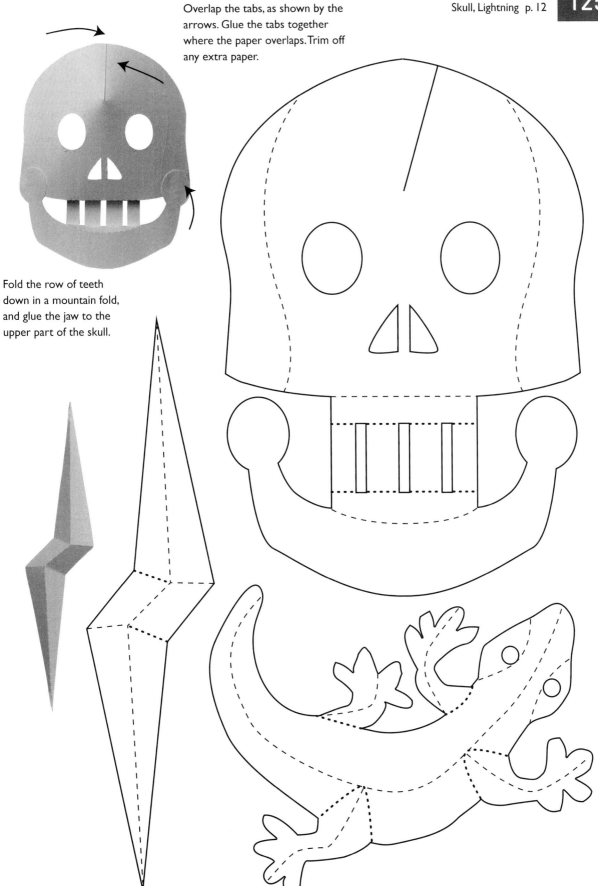

Overlap the tabs, as shown by the arrows. Glue the tabs together where the paper overlaps. Trim off any extra paper.

Fold the row of teeth down in a mountain fold, and glue the jaw to the upper part of the skull.

Sword, Iron Bars,
Thorns, Bones p. 12

125%

Sword p. 12

Crown 2 p. 12

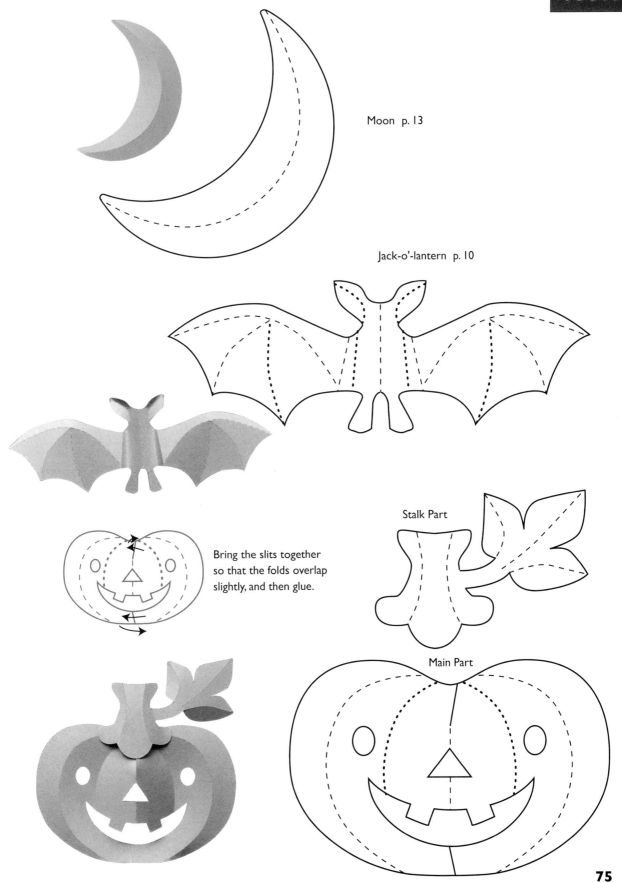

Moon p.13

Jack-o'-lantern p.10

Bring the slits together
so that the folds overlap
slightly, and then glue.

Stalk Part

Main Part

Letters are small, so it's best to use a ballpoint pen to make creases. These patterns are inverted so that you can make sharper folds at the creases. Be careful not to turn the letters upside down or backward.

The dotted line shown here indicates the folded reliefs. Try folding the mountain folds while looking at the photograph of the finished piece.

Decorative Alphabet p. 14

Poster Board

Art Paper (back side)

Pattern

Turn the letter over to make the creases.

If the valley folds are hard to fold, use a ballpoint pen to make perforations on the front side once again.

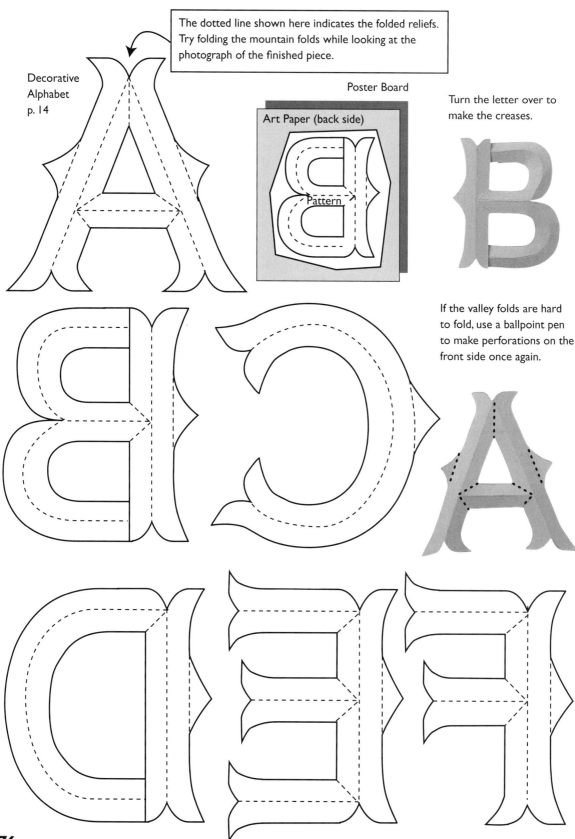

① Make creases in the
   paper.
② Fold A and B together
   toward the middle,
   then glue A to B.

A

B

Gluing
Tab

③ Make a crease in the middle of A by
   pushing the two sides together.

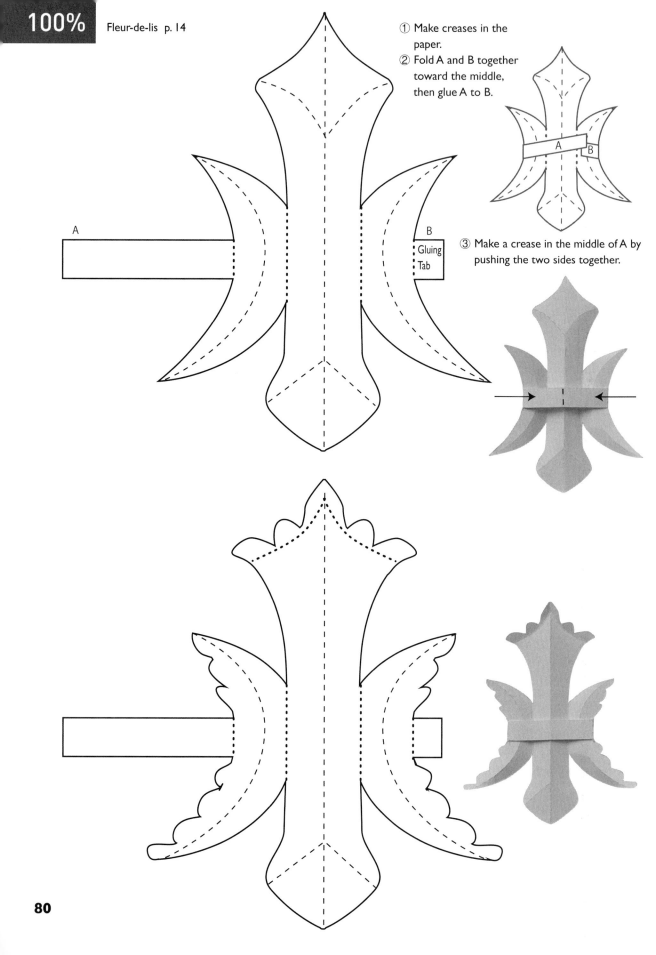

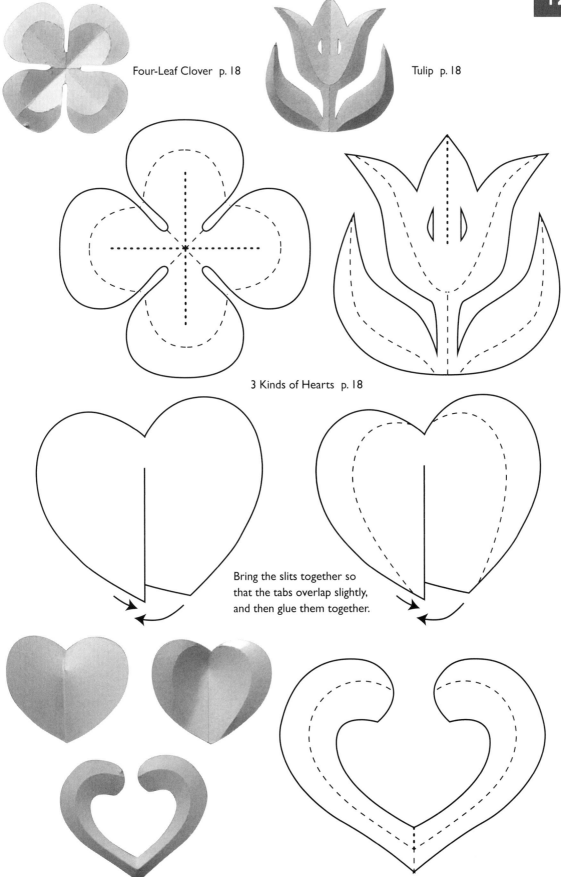

Four-Leaf Clover p. 18

Tulip p. 18

3 Kinds of Hearts p. 18

Bring the slits together so
that the tabs overlap slightly,
and then glue them together.

Simple Flowers p. 18

Ducks p. 19

Rabbits p. 19

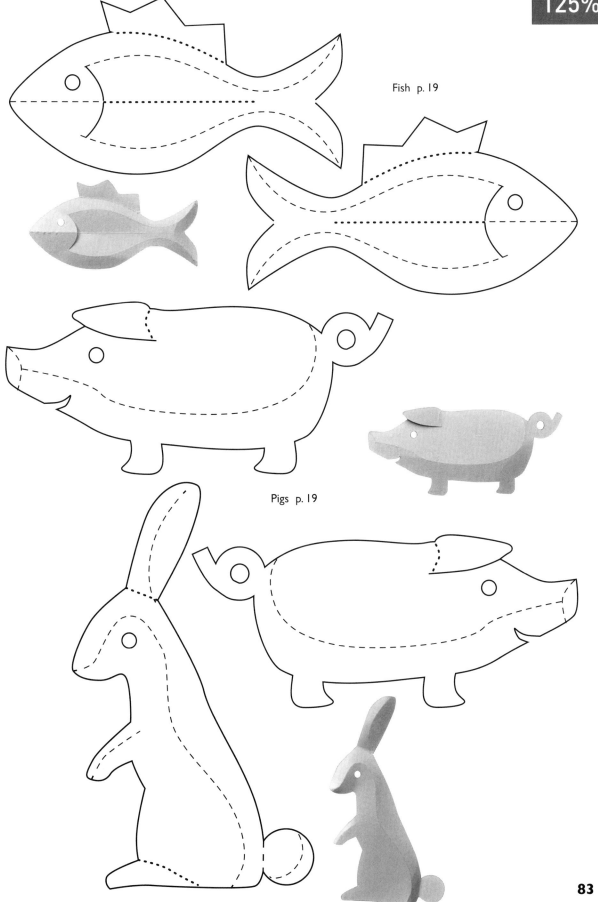

Fish p. 19

Pigs p. 19

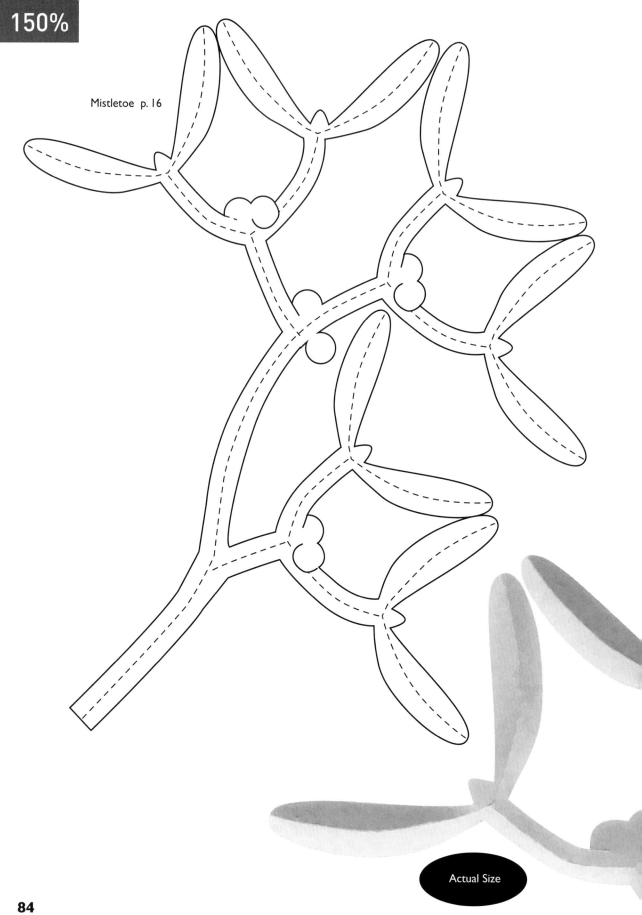

Mistletoe p. 16

Actual Size

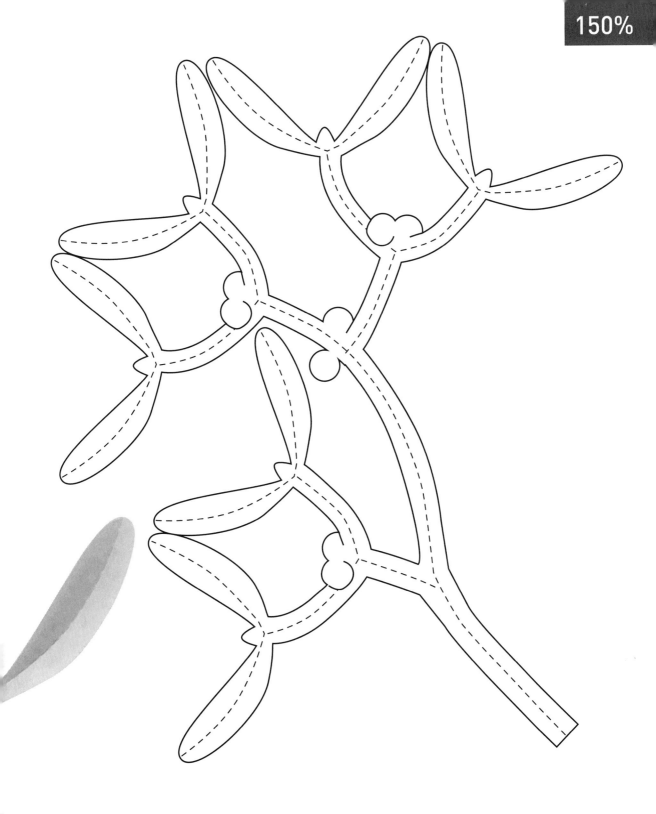

Plain Alphabet p. 20

Letters are small, so use a ballpoint pen to make creases. These patterns are inverted so that you can make sharper folds at the creases. Be careful not to turn the letters upside down or backward. Refer to pages 58 and 76.

The dotted line shown here indicates the folded reliefs. Try folding the mountain folds while looking at the photograph of the finished piece.

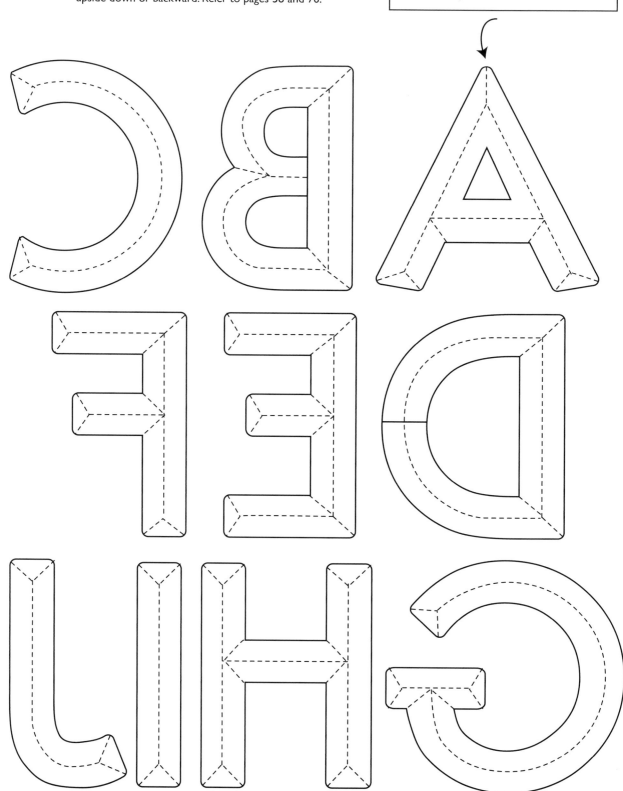

Flowers and Leaves for
Vases p. 22

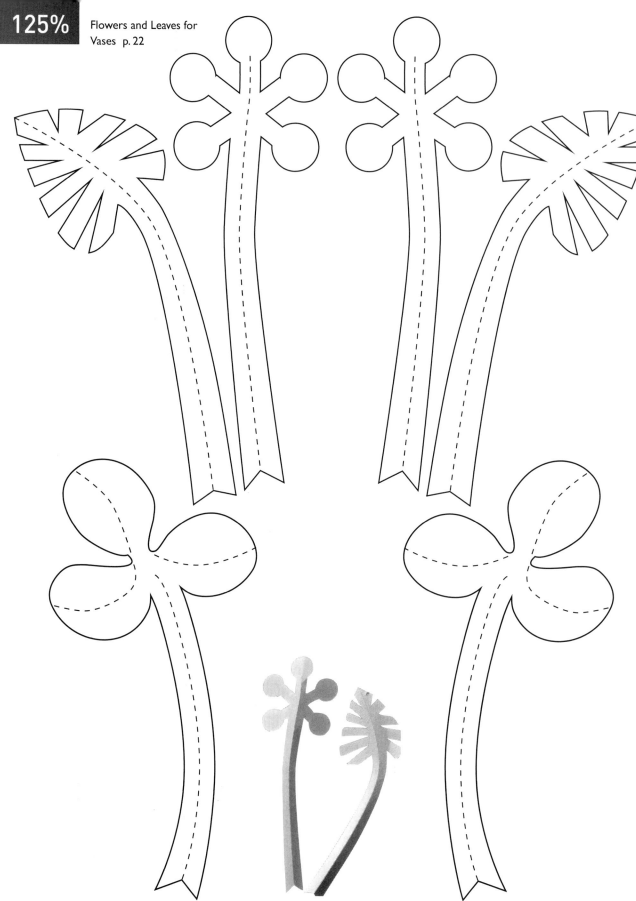

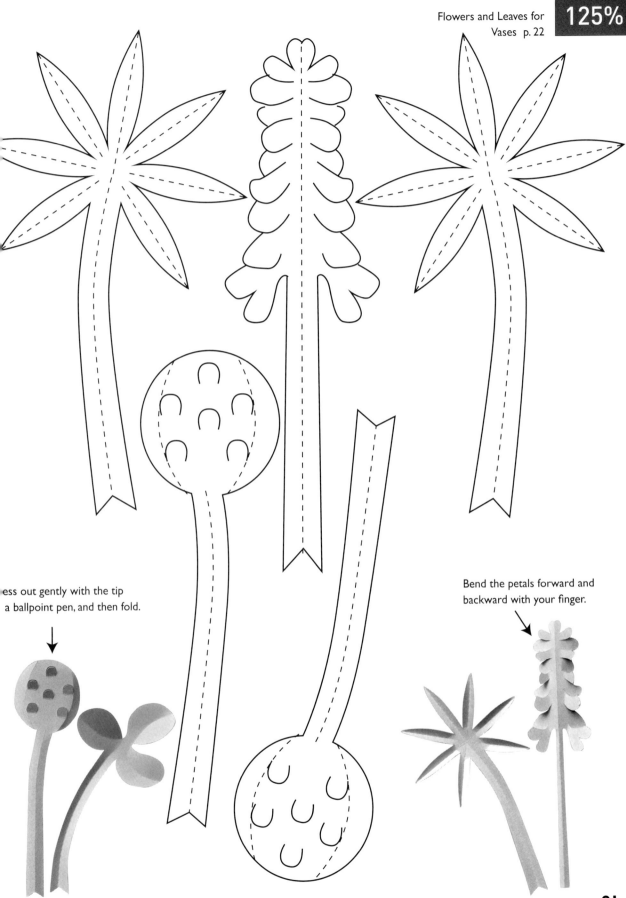

ess out gently with the tip
a ballpoint pen, and then fold.

Bend the petals forward and
backward with your finger.

Flowers and Leaves for
Vases p. 22

For leaves, use either side
as the front.

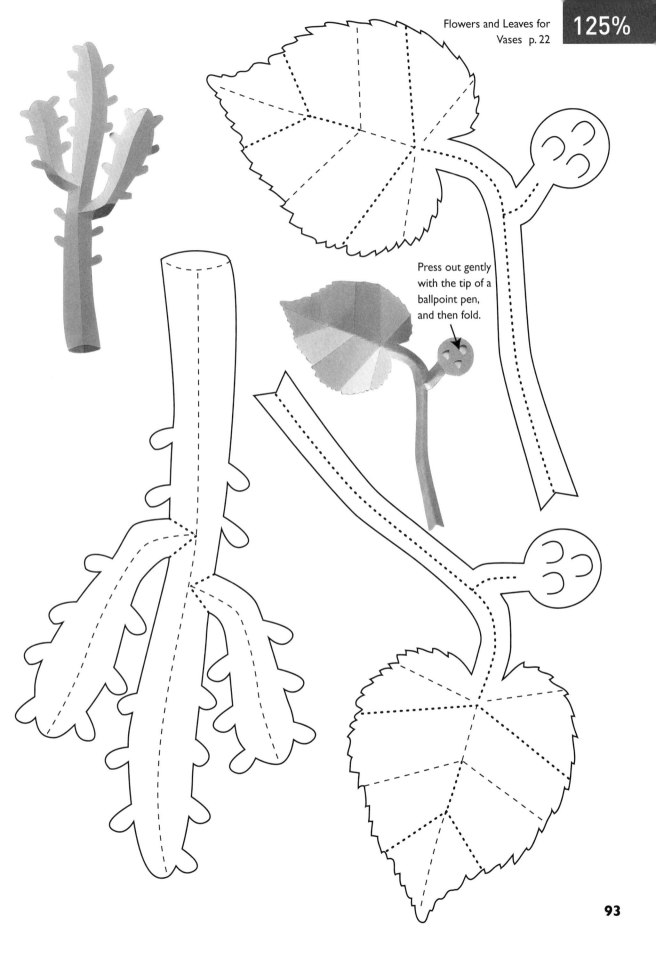

Press out gently
with the tip of a
ballpoint pen,
and then fold.

Flowers and Leaves for
Vases p. 22

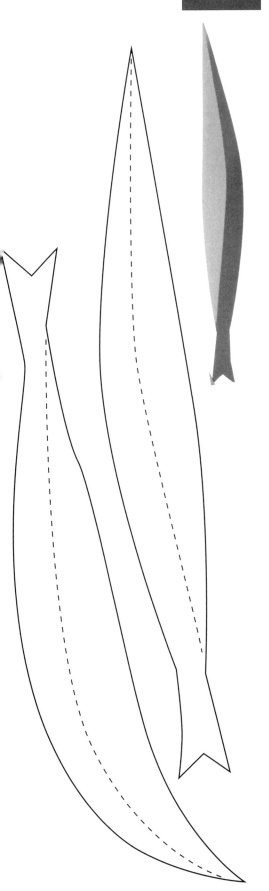

Lily of the Valley Basket p. 24
Flower Basket p. 25

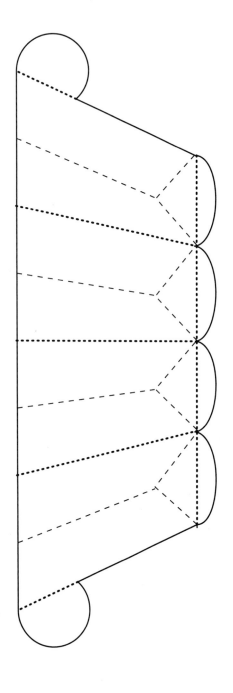

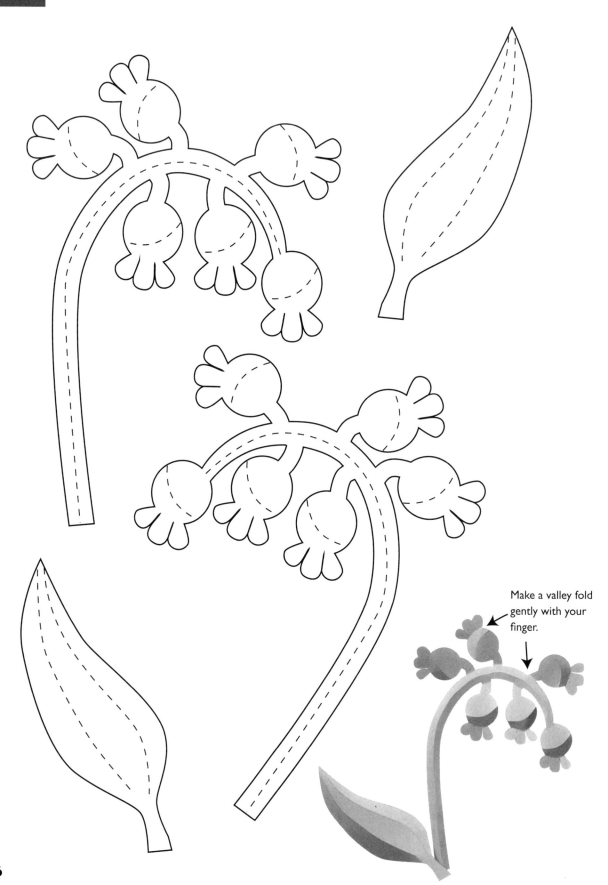

Make a valley fold gently with your finger.

Fold creases at the tabs around the center.

Cut out the
gray area.

Overlap the petals slightly at the slit, and glue.

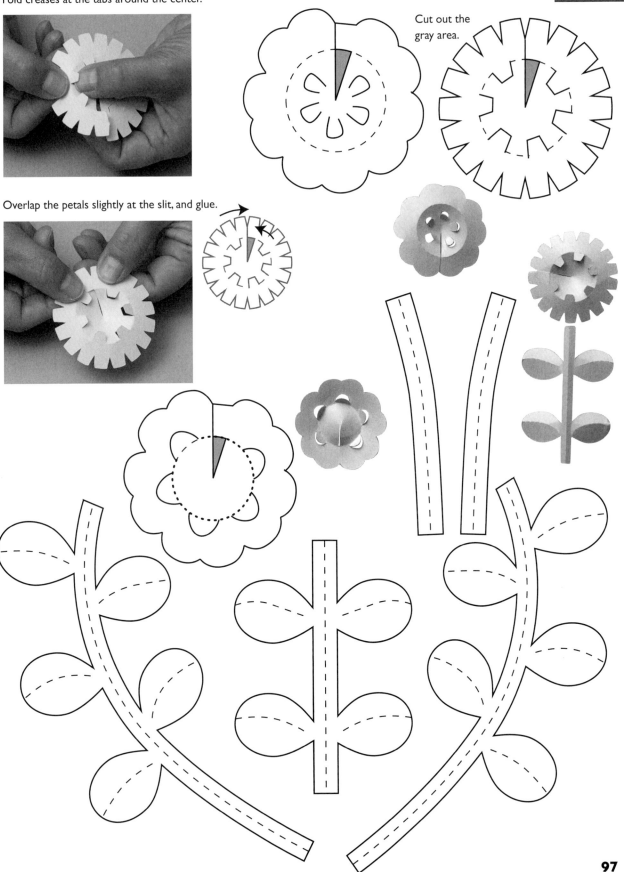

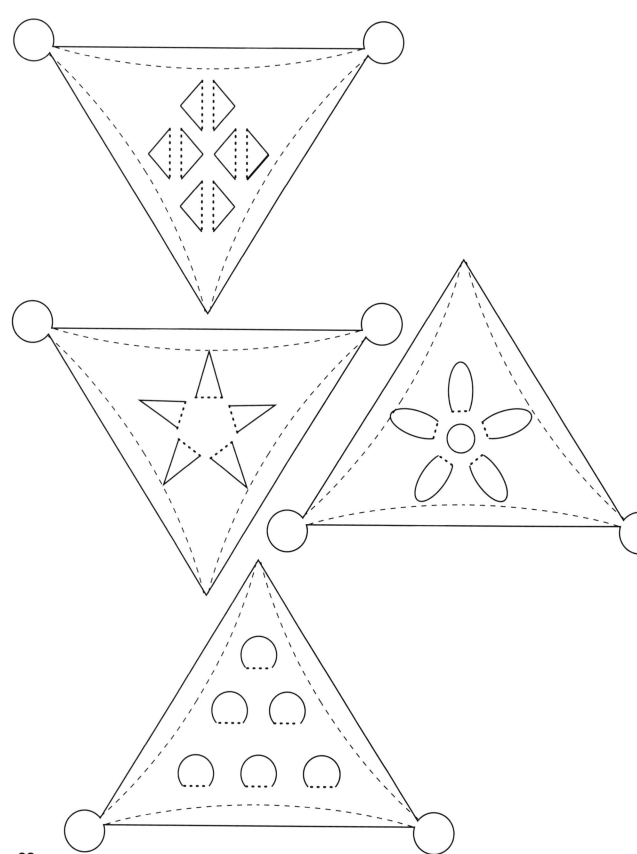

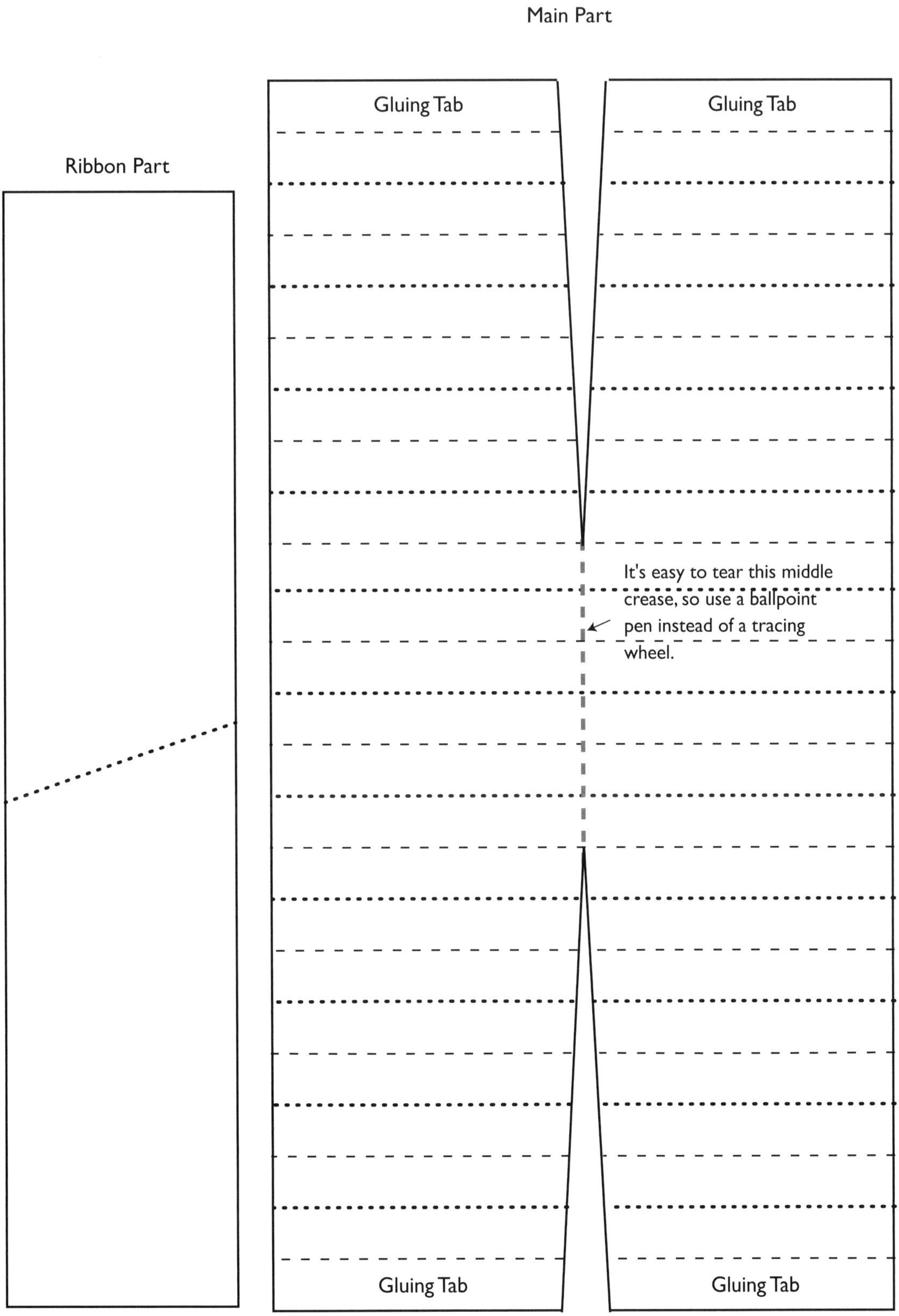

Main Part

Ribbon Part

Gluing Tab

Gluing Tab

It's easy to tear this middle crease, so use a ballpoint pen instead of a tracing wheel.

Gluing Tab

Gluing Tab

① Fold the Main Part into mountain and valley folds, like an accordion. Bring the Gluing Tabs together, and glue.

② Fold the ribbon, and attach it to the back of the Main Part.

③ Stick the Circular Part to the Main Part, and attach letters and numbers with glue.

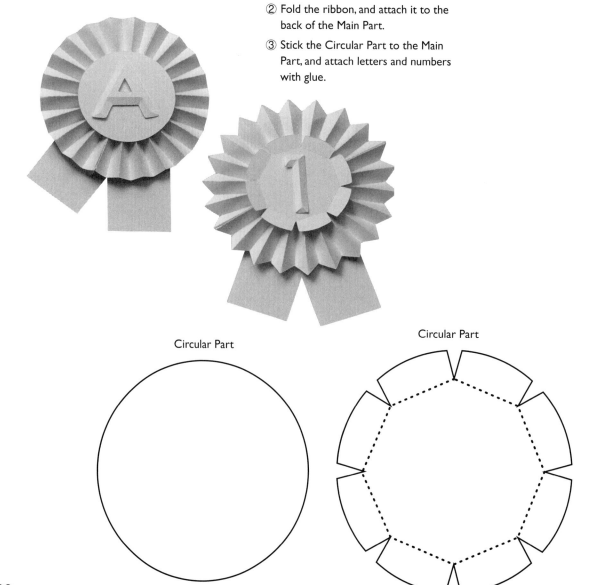

Circular Part

Circular Part

Main Part

Ribbon Part

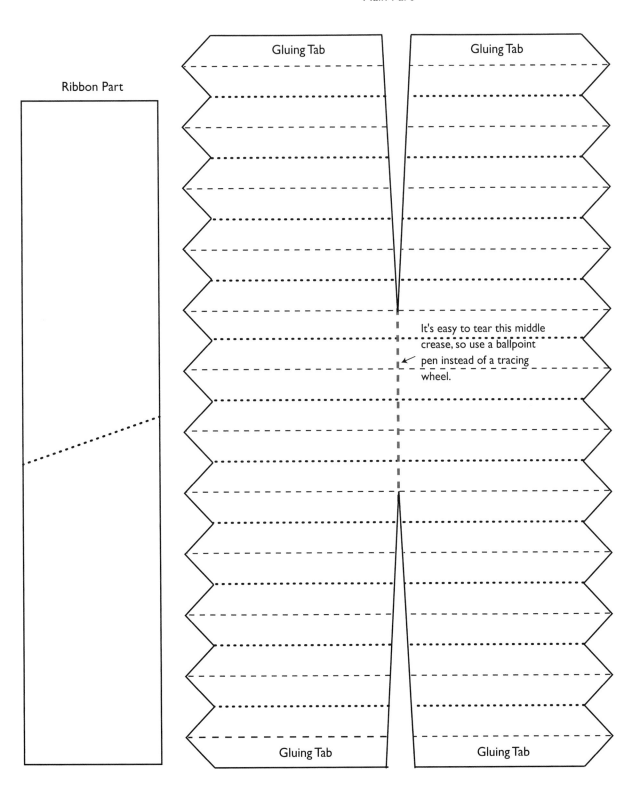

Gluing Tab

Gluing Tab

It's easy to tear this middle crease, so use a ballpoint pen instead of a tracing wheel.

Gluing Tab

Gluing Tab

Rose p. 28

Climbing Rose p. 28

Please refer to p. 59
to make creases for
the flowers.

Rose p. 28

Climbing Rose p. 28

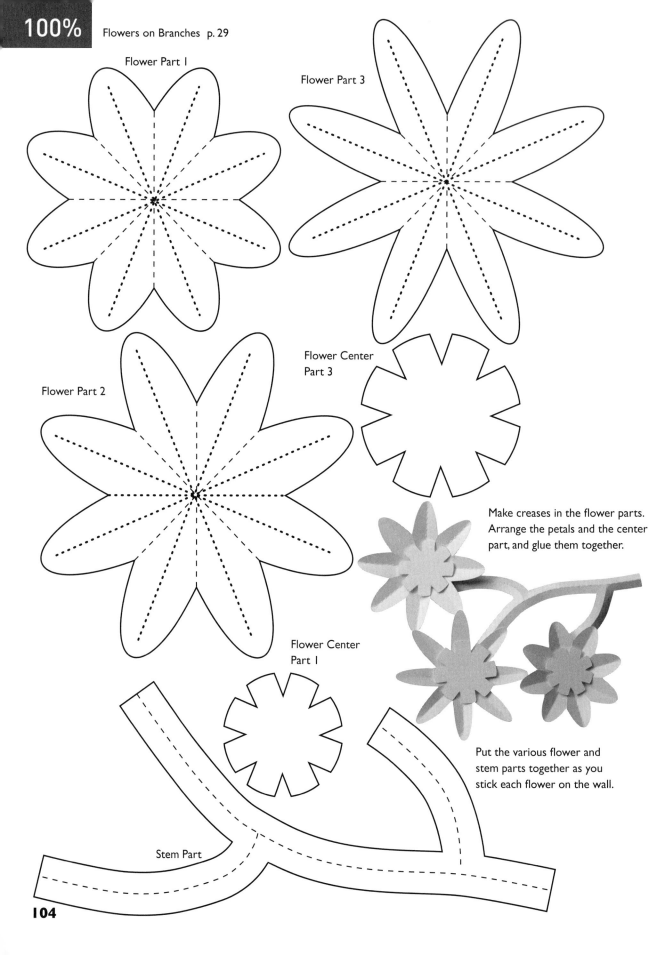

Flower Part 1

Flower Part 3

Flower Part 2

Flower Center
Part 3

Make creases in the flower parts.
Arrange the petals and the center
part, and glue them together.

Flower Center
Part 1

Put the various flower and
stem parts together as you
stick each flower on the wall.

Stem Part

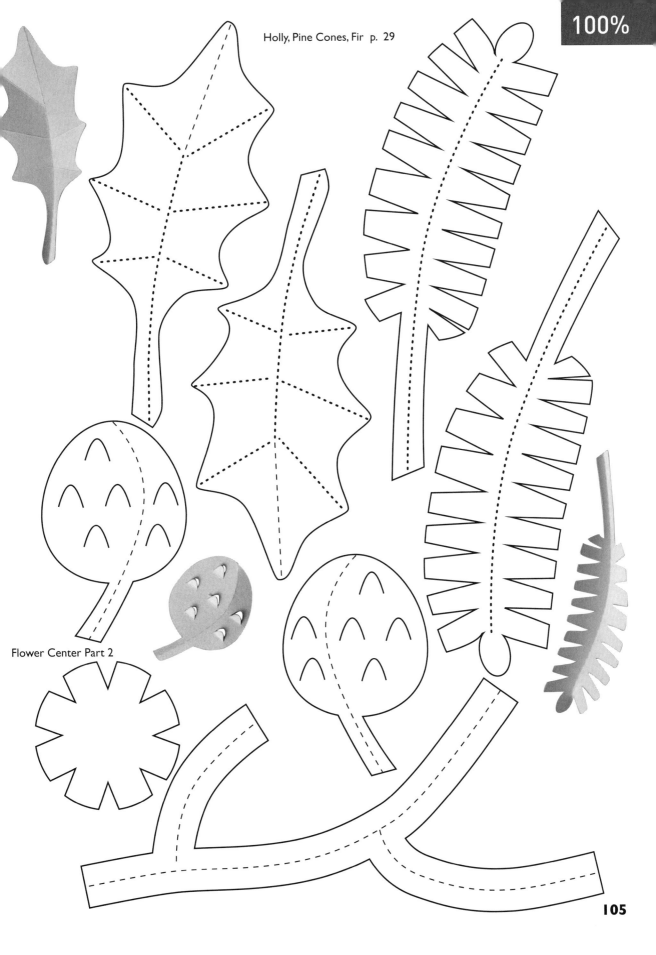

Flower Center Part 2

Peapods p. 17

For Peapods, please refer to the
basic techniques on pp. 51–57.

Apples, Pears p. 30
Oranges p. 30

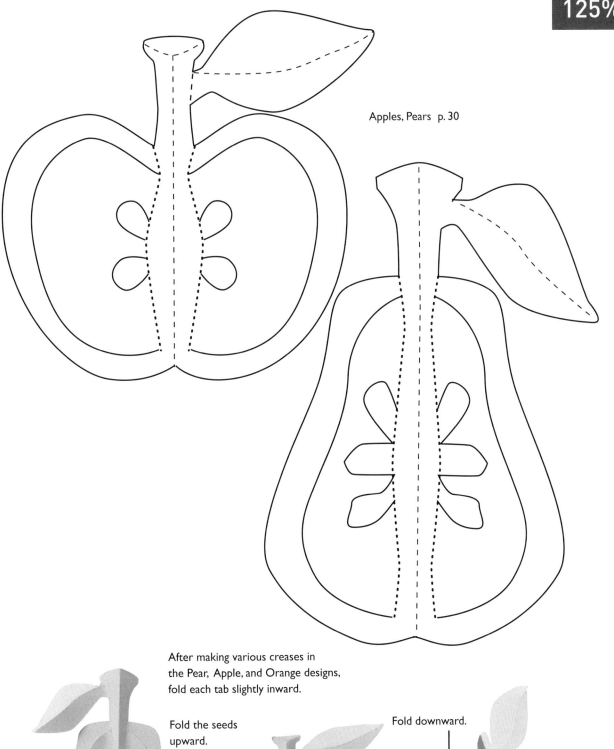

Apples, Pears p. 30

After making various creases in
the Pear, Apple, and Orange designs,
fold each tab slightly inward.

Fold the seeds
upward.

Fold downward.

107

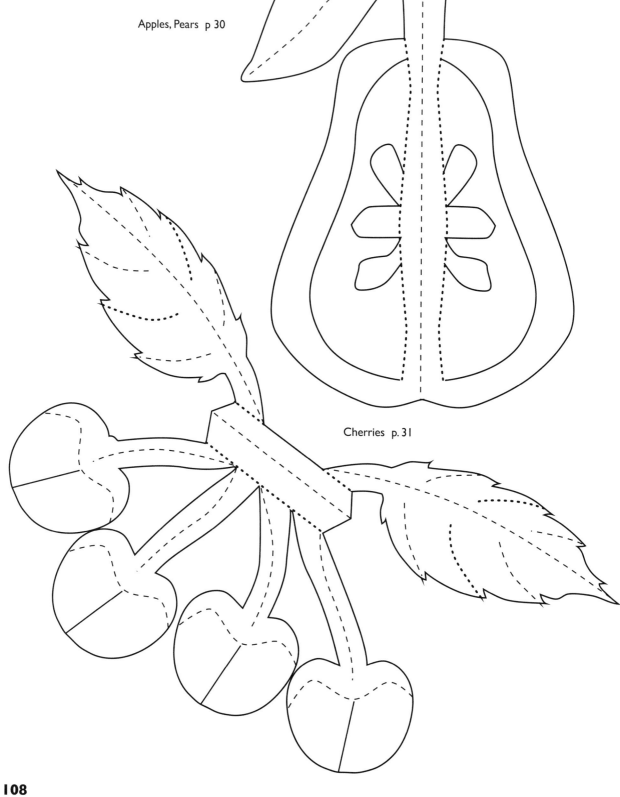

Apples, Pears p 30

Cherries p. 31

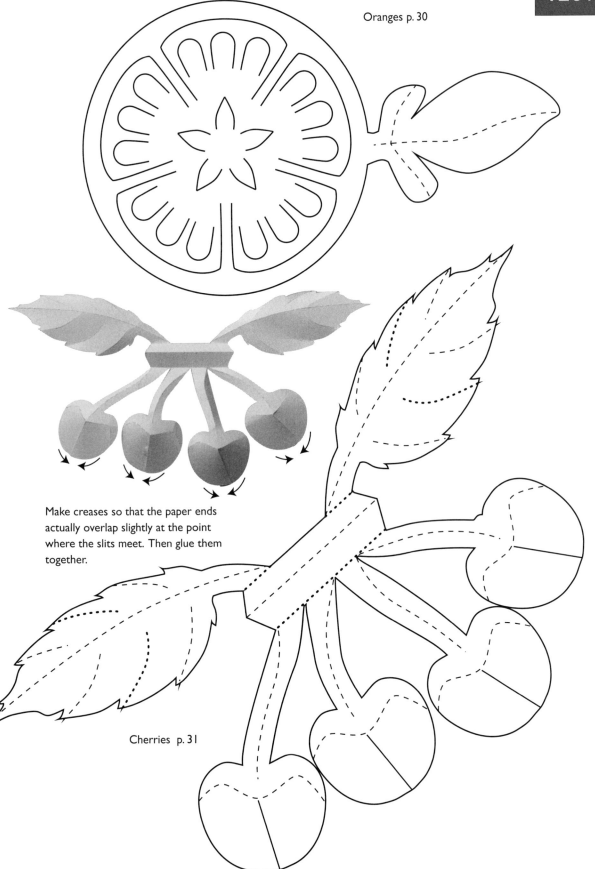

Oranges p. 30

Make creases so that the paper ends
actually overlap slightly at the point
where the slits meet. Then glue them
together.

Cherries p. 31

Stem Part

Vine Part

Grape Parts

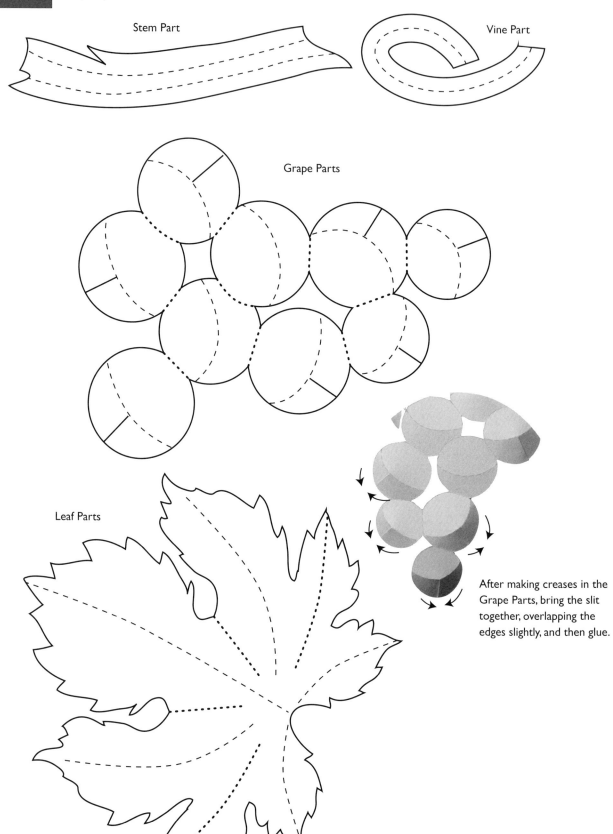

Leaf Parts

After making creases in the Grape Parts, bring the slit together, overlapping the edges slightly, and then glue.

125%

Vine Part

Stem Part

Grape Parts

Put the various parts together as
you stick each one on the wall.

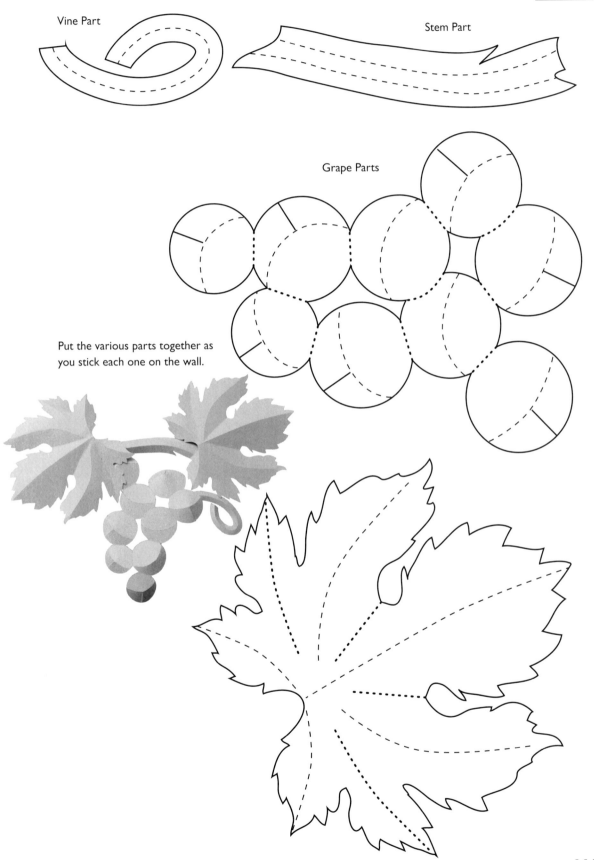

Thread a string through a hole punched with an awl or a hole punch.

Write your message before creasing and folding.

For the leaf design, bend the leaf cutout with your finger and glue the tip to the tag slightly off-center.

Happy Birthday

Thank you!

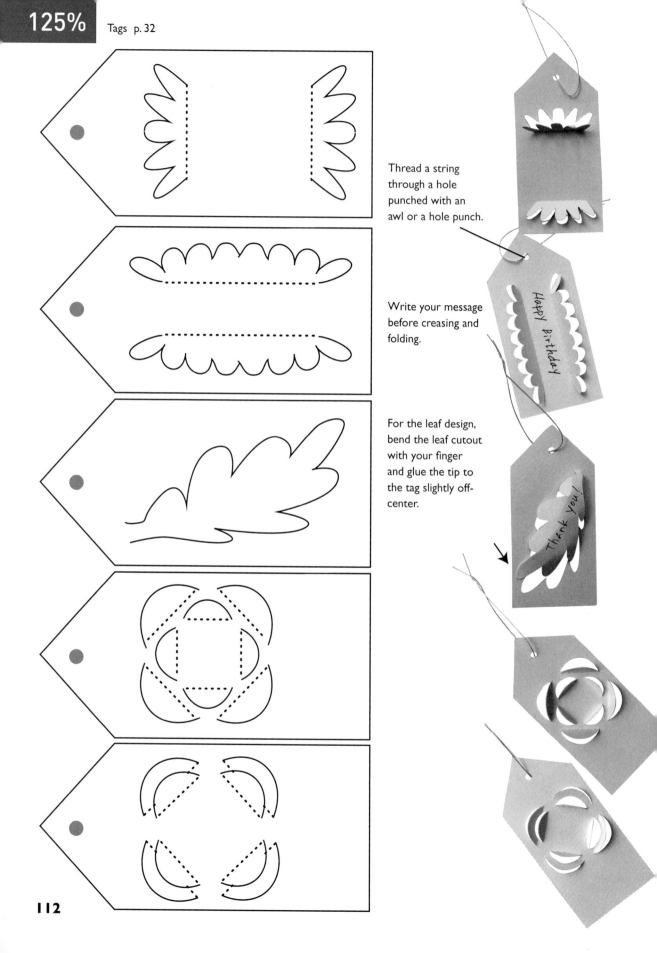

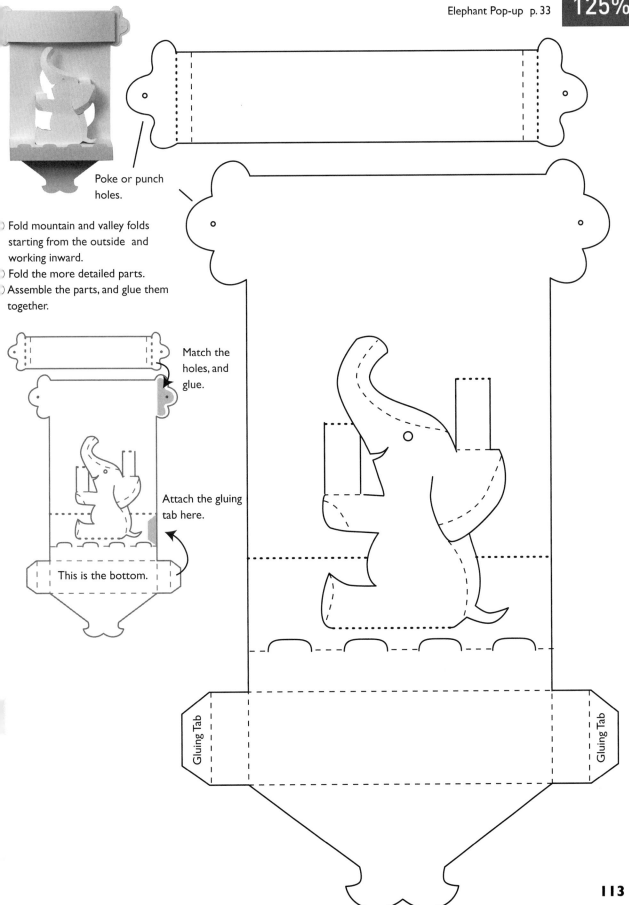

Poke or punch holes.

) Fold mountain and valley folds starting from the outside and working inward.
) Fold the more detailed parts.
) Assemble the parts, and glue them together.

Match the holes, and glue.

Attach the gluing tab here.

This is the bottom.

Gluing Tab

Gluing Tab

Cut out and fold toward the center.

Attach a small amount of wedge-shaped adhesive to the back of the wing, and stick it to the wall.

Do not make perforations when making the creases for the softest crease edges. Punch a round hole with a hole punch.

Mobile p. 34

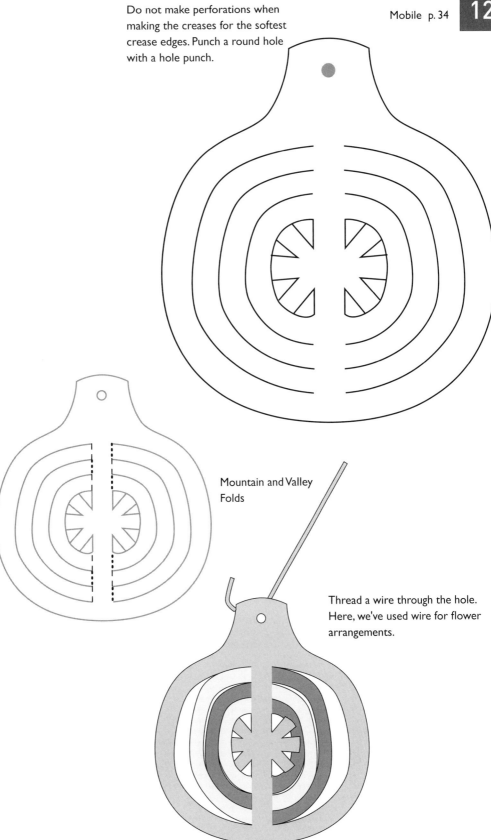

Mountain and Valley Folds

Thread a wire through the hole. Here, we've used wire for flower arrangements.

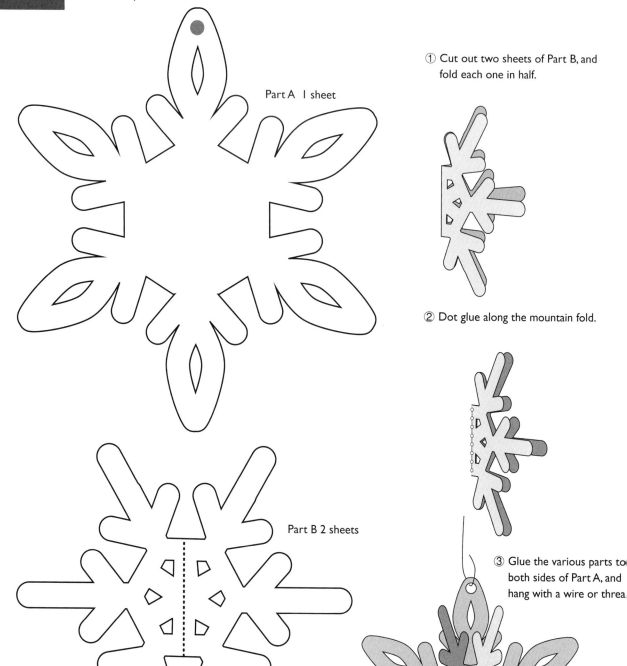

Part A 1 sheet

Part B 2 sheets

① Cut out two sheets of Part B, and fold each one in half.

② Dot glue along the mountain fold.

③ Glue the various parts to both sides of Part A, and hang with a wire or threa

How to Make Cubic Shapes

Make creases with a ballpoint pen, and fold. Since there are many mountain folds, we have inverted the pattern paper. Please look at the photograph of the finished shape as you put it together.

The dotted lines show where to make a crease.

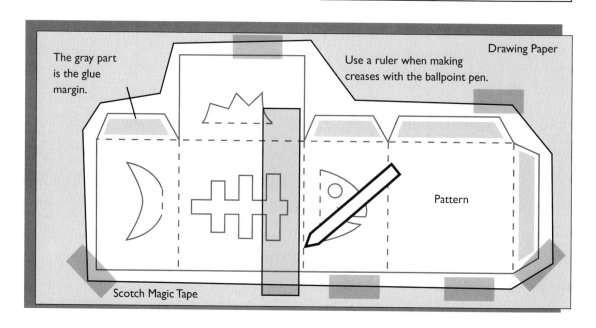

The gray part is the glue margin.

Use a ruler when making creases with the ballpoint pen.

Drawing Paper

Pattern

Scotch Magic Tape

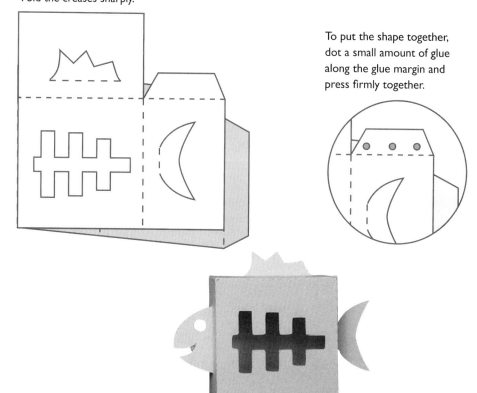

Fold the creases sharply.

To put the shape together, dot a small amount of glue along the glue margin and press firmly together.

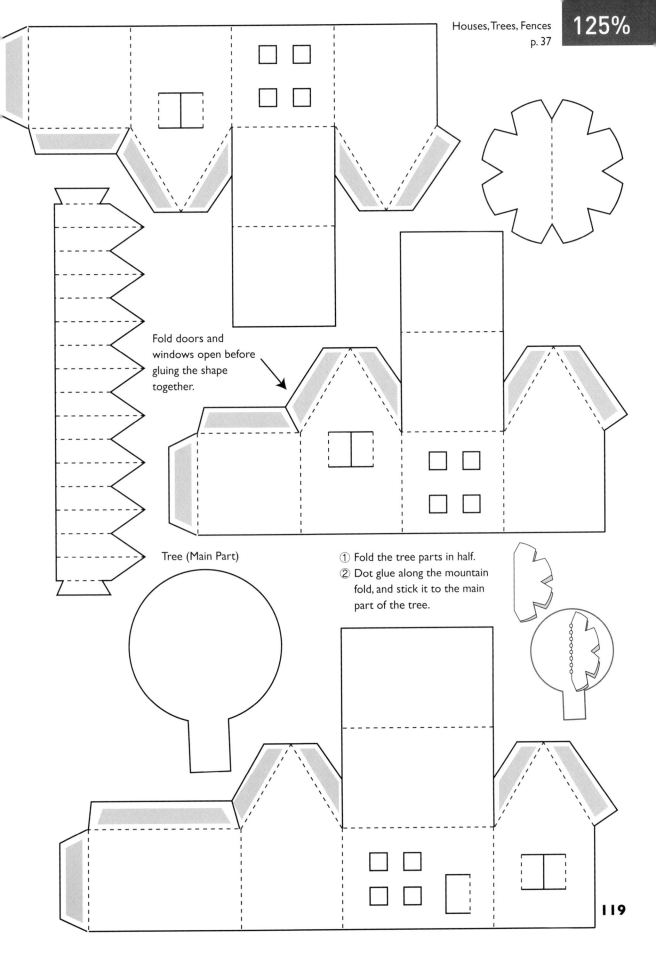

Fold doors and
windows open before
gluing the shape
together.

Tree (Main Part)

① Fold the tree parts in half.
② Dot glue along the mountain
   fold, and stick it to the main
   part of the tree.

119

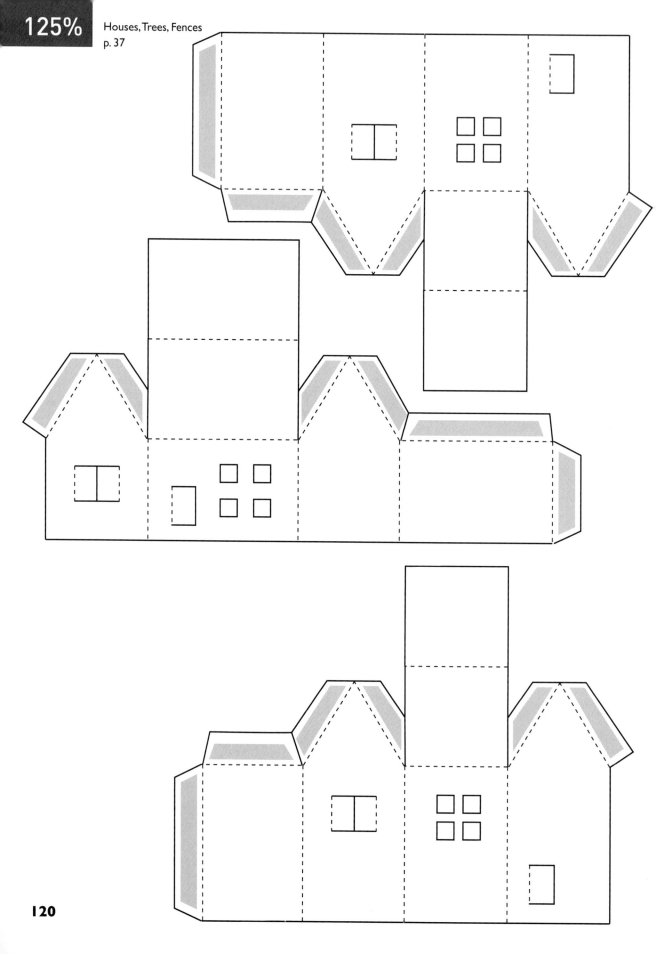

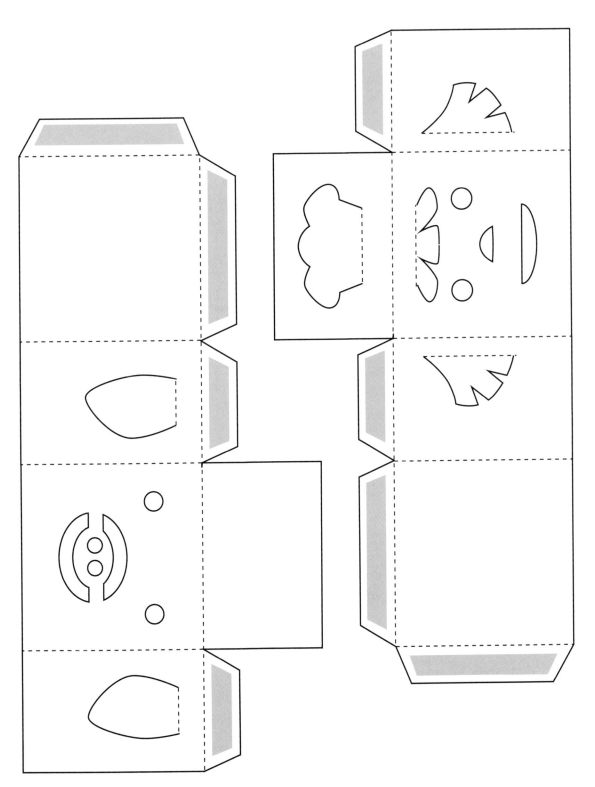

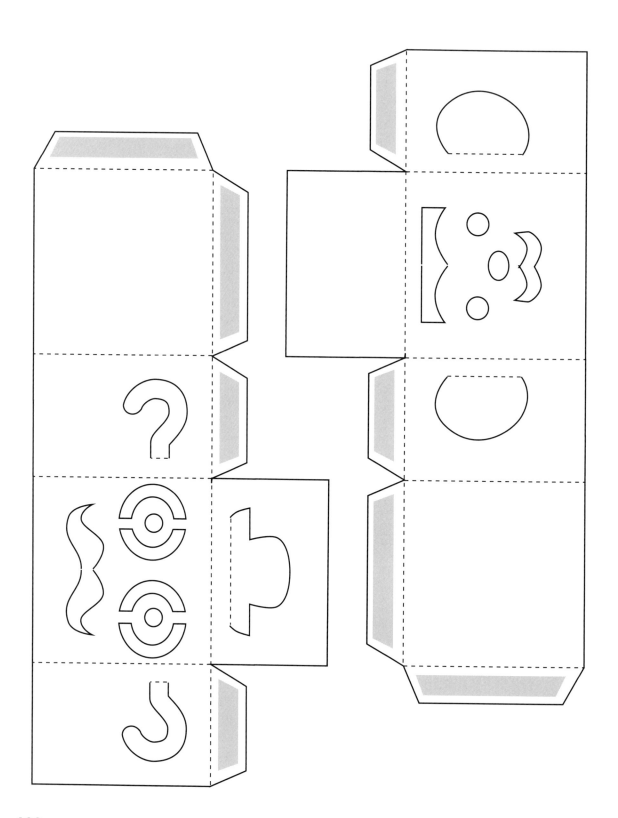

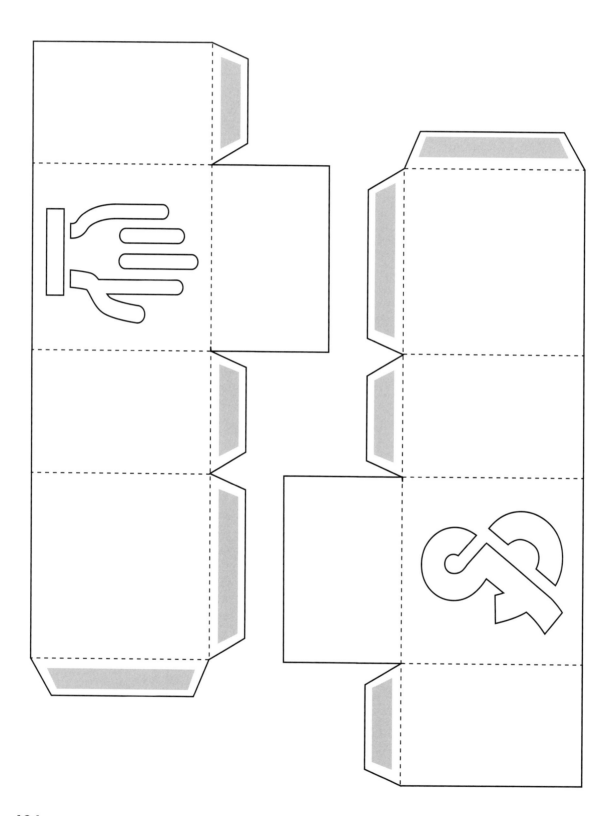

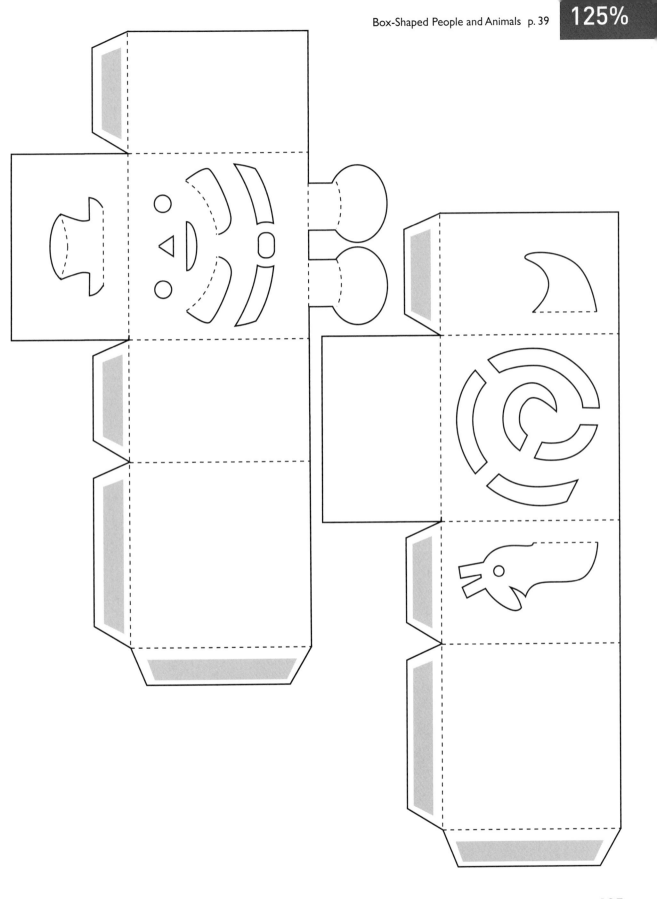

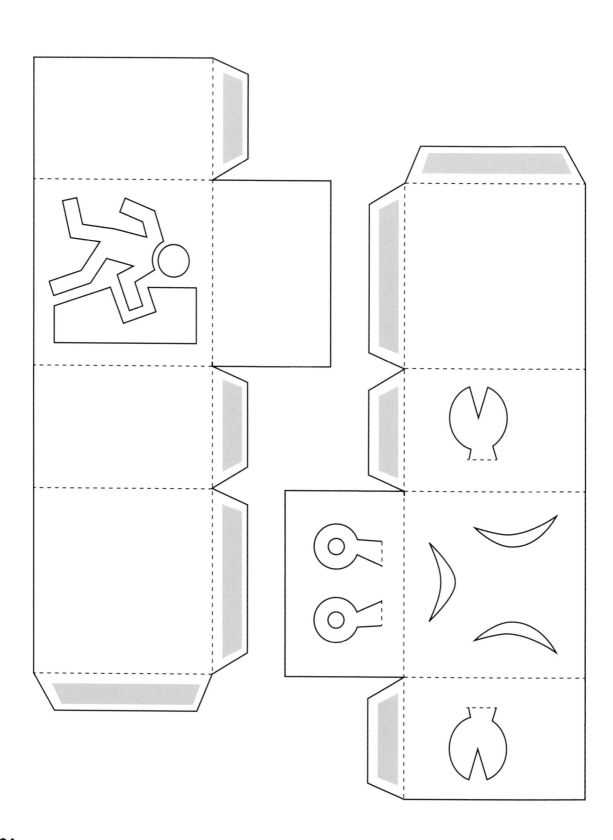

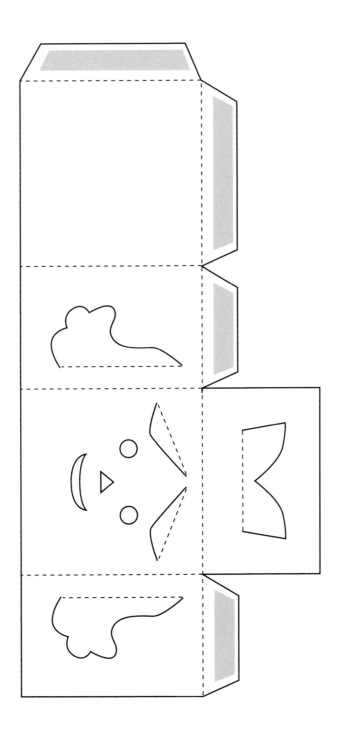

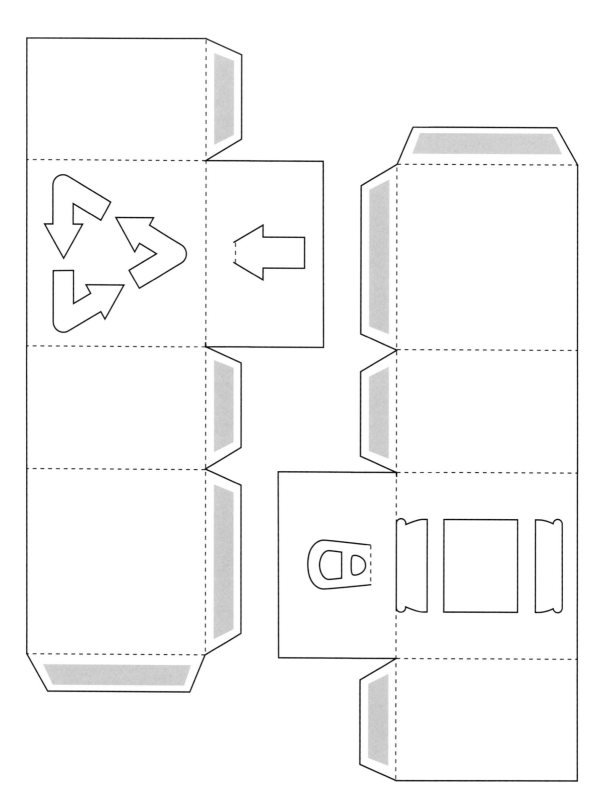

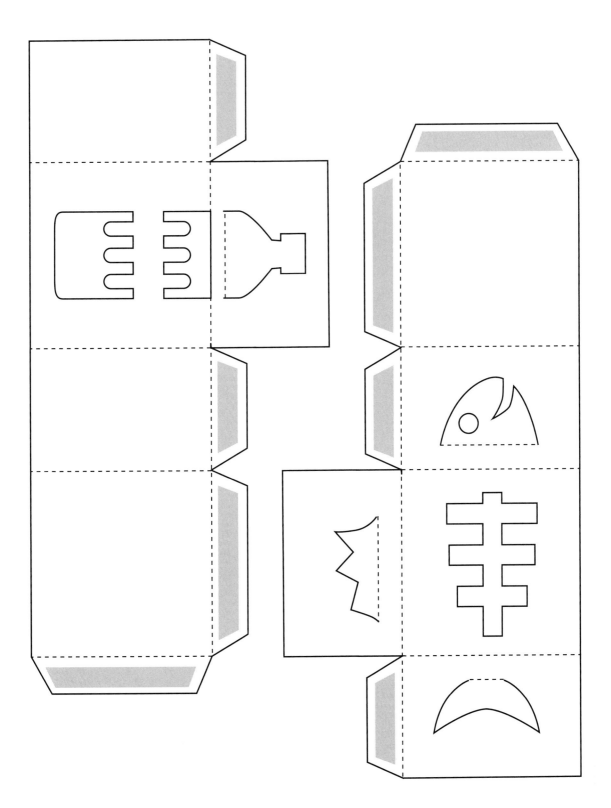

Since there are many mountain folds, make creases on the reverse side of the pattern with a ballpoint pen to make folding easier. Refer to the photos of the finished letters as you work to make sure you don't make them backward.

The dotted lines show where to make the creases.

Cardboard

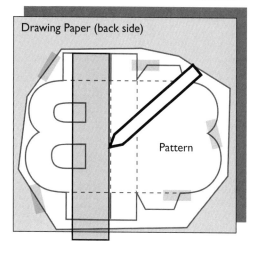

Drawing Paper (back side)

Pattern

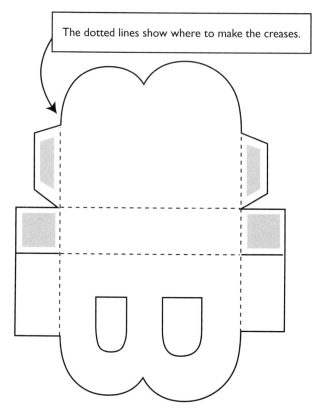

Turn the paper over and assemble.
Look at the photograph of the completed letter as you are folding the pieces together.

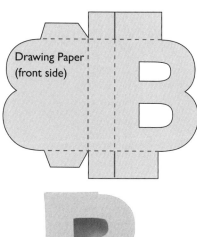

Drawing Paper (front side)

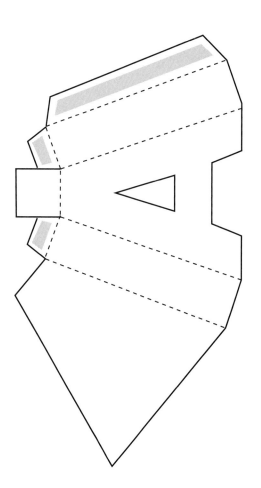

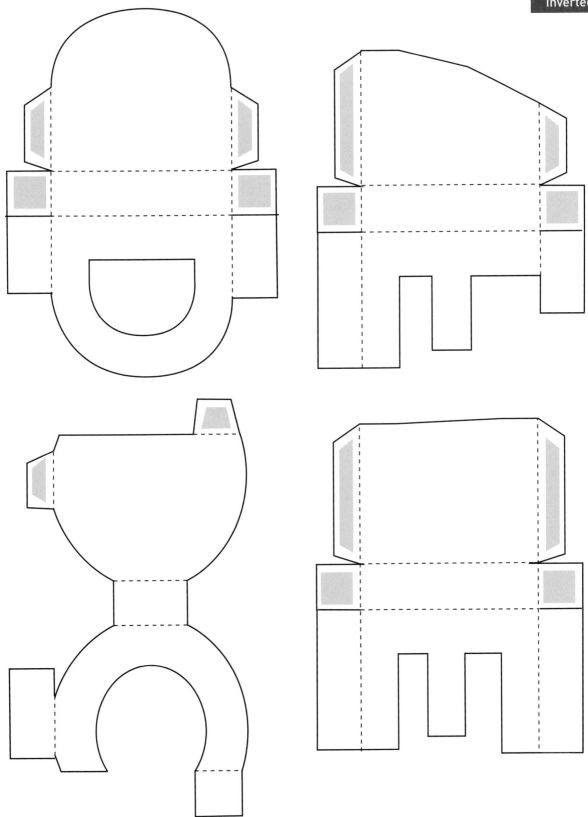

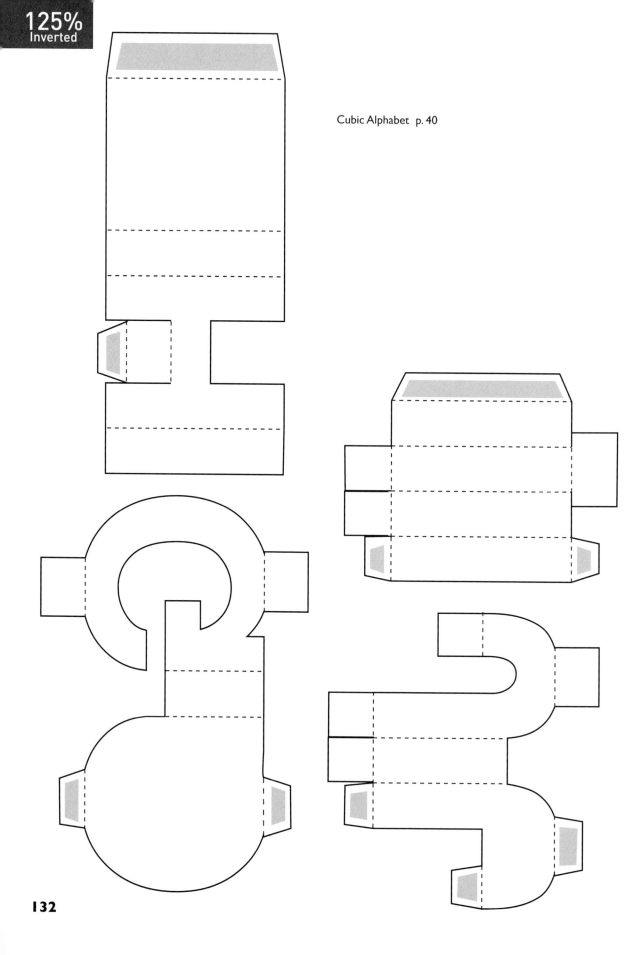

Cubic Alphabet p. 40

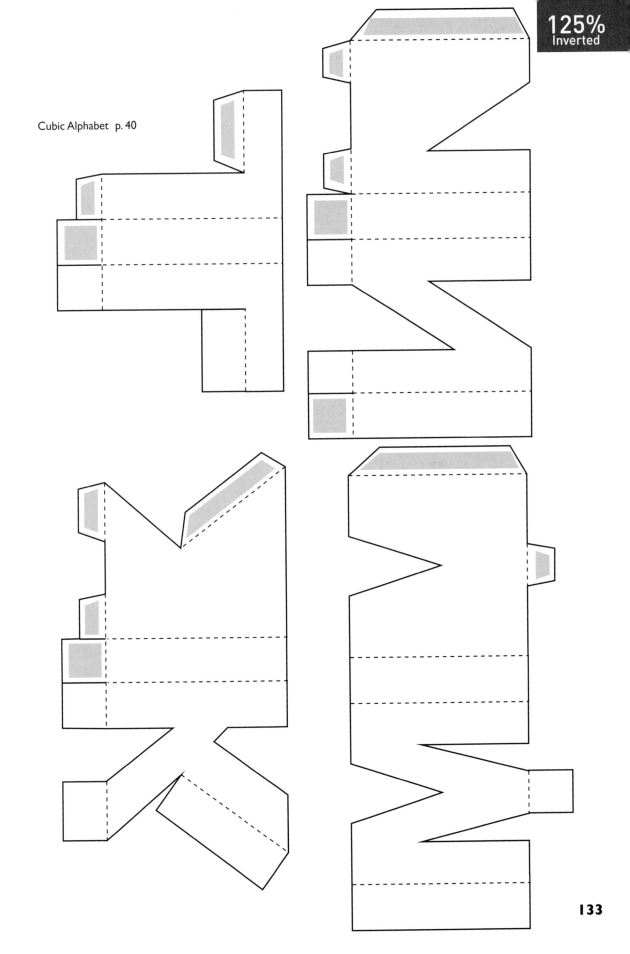

Cubic Alphabet p. 40

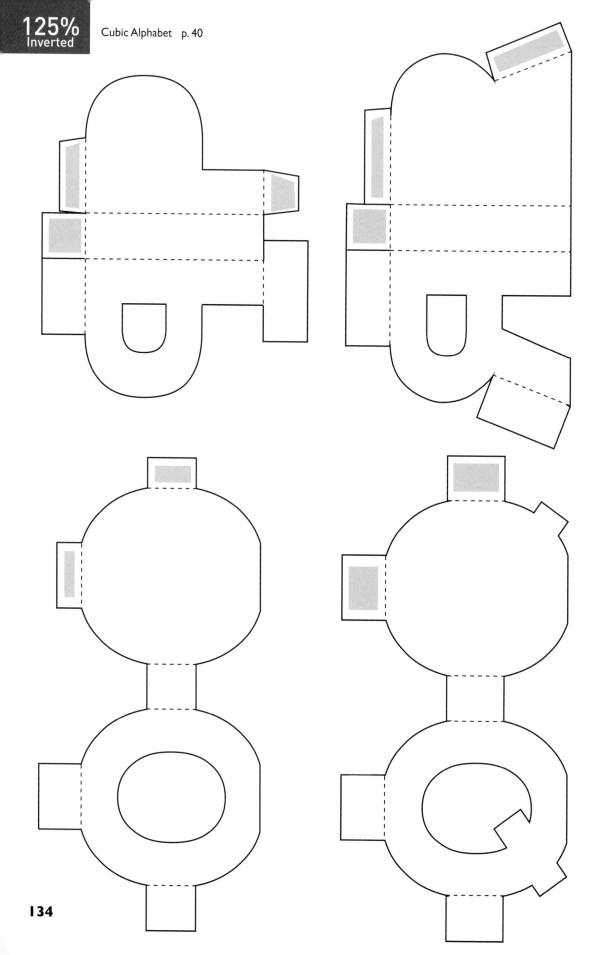

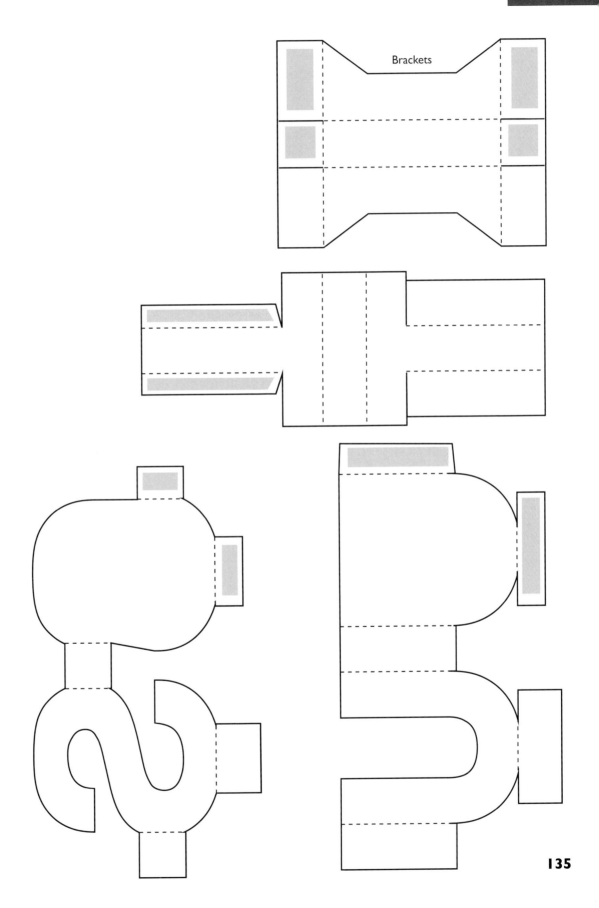

Brackets

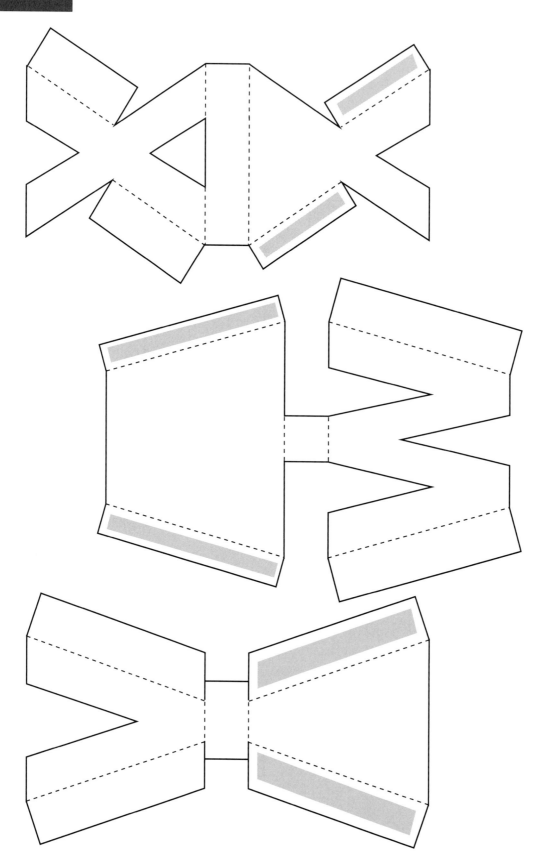

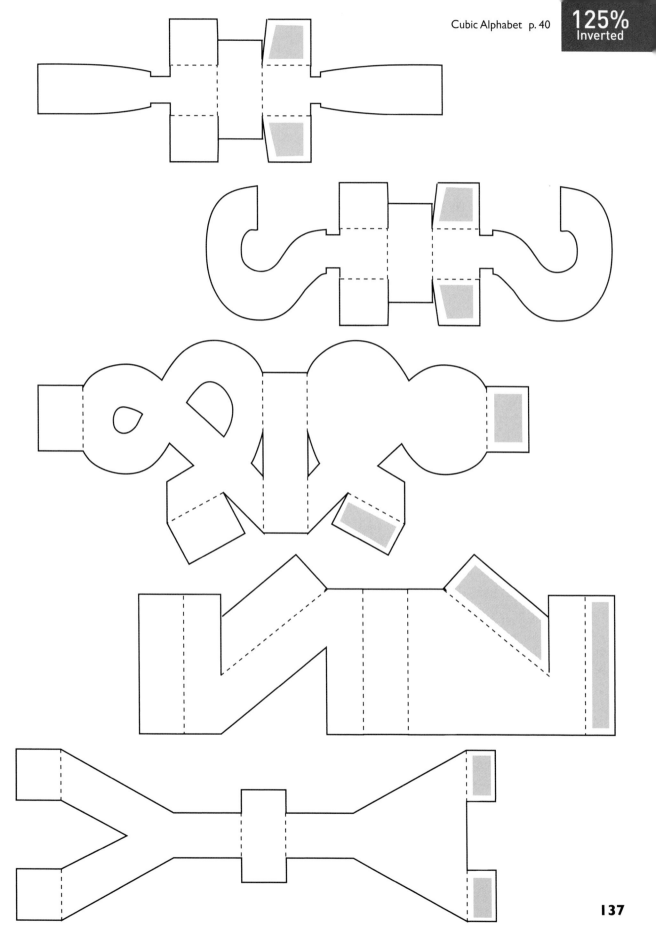

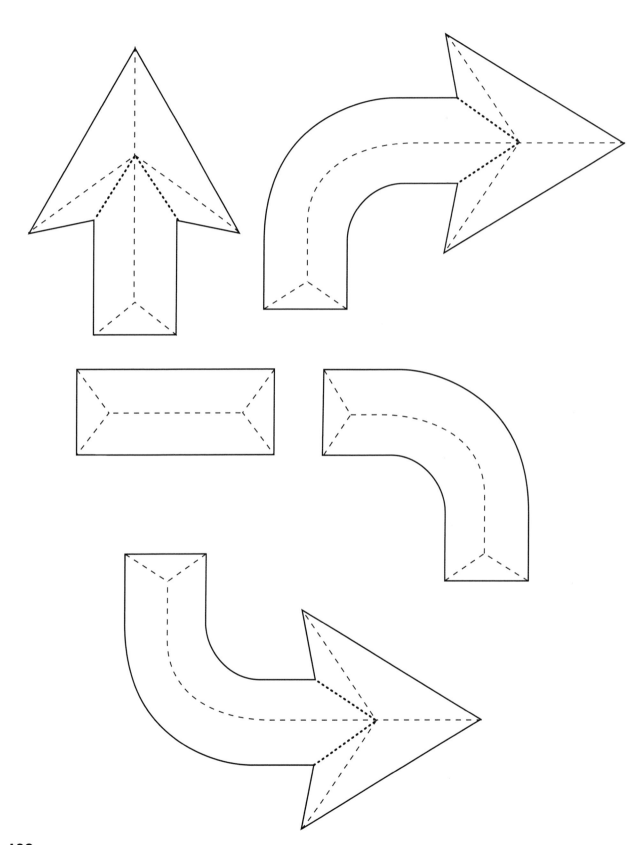

← Top

Fold along the dotted line to put the rack together.
Insert the end tabs at the bottom into the slit.

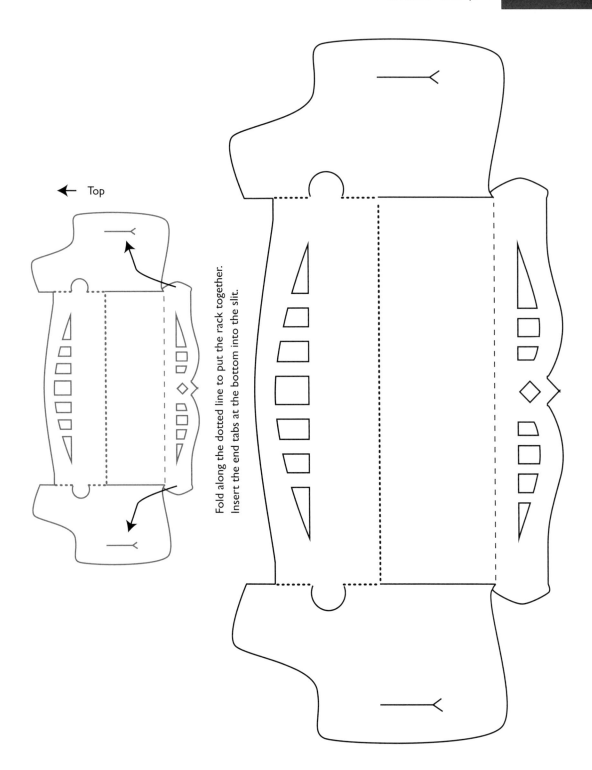

Wall Racks, Hooks p. 42

These designs can be made in three different sizes.

① Fold along the dotted line, and put it together.
② Stick A to B.
③ Stick C to B.
④ Stick D to E.

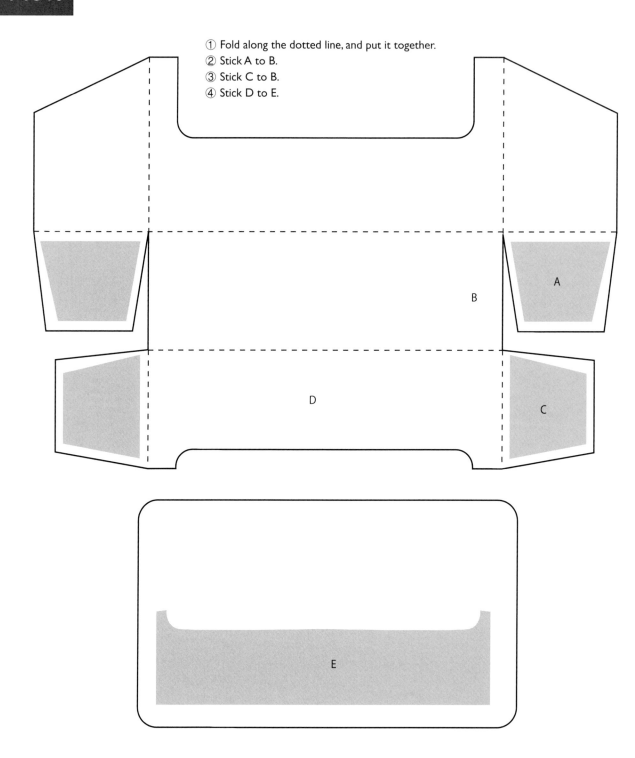

Make a mountain fold along
the dotted line. Apply adhesive
to the gray parts, and stick
them together.

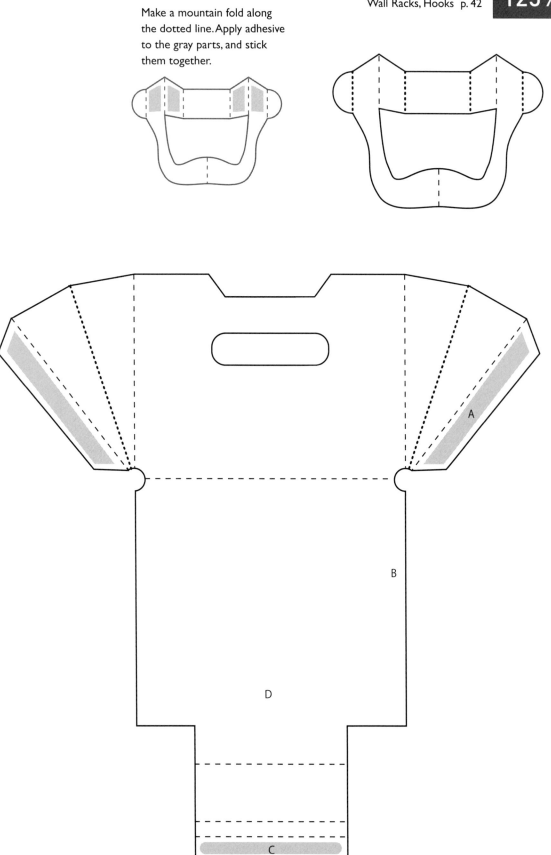

A

B

D

C

This pattern is made to fit paper cups.

Approximately 2 1/8" (5.5 cm)

Approximately
2 3/8" (6 cm)

① Fold and assemble, as shown
   in the diagram.
② Stick A to B.
③ Stick C to D.
④ Insert the paper cup.

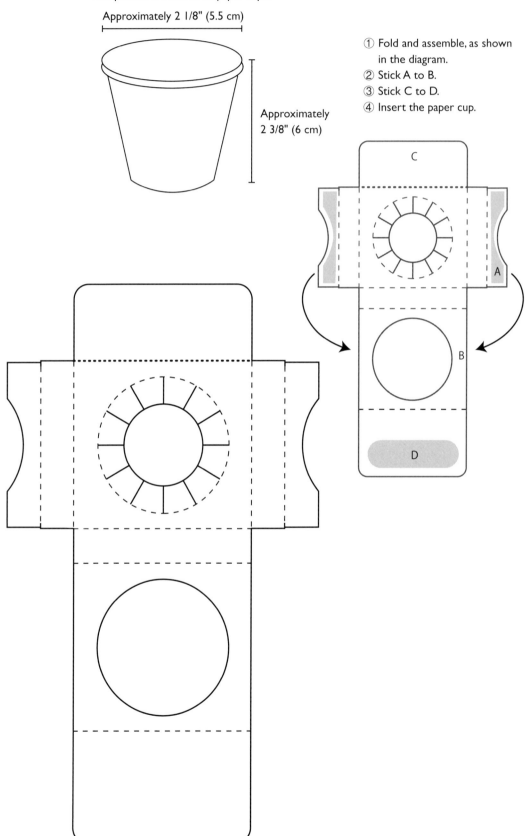

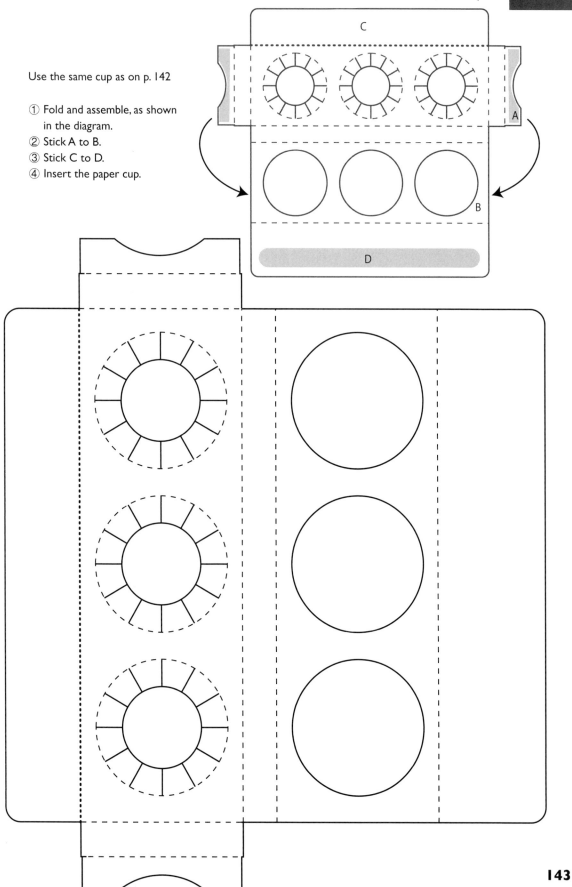

Use the same cup as on p. 142

① Fold and assemble, as shown
   in the diagram.
② Stick A to B.
③ Stick C to D.
④ Insert the paper cup.

① Apply adhesive to each of the tips of paper, and attach them to the main part of the basket.
② Stick the tips down one at a time. Then attach the handles.

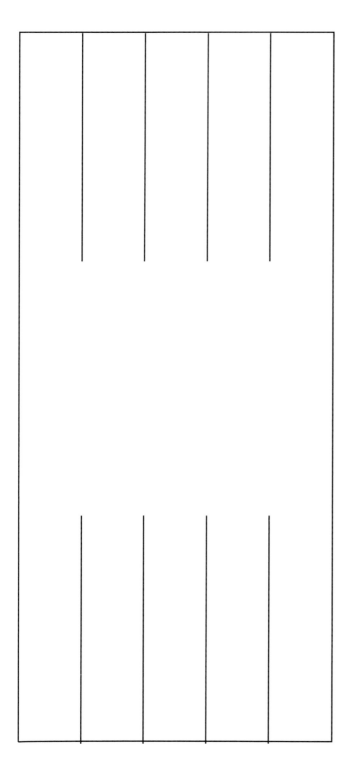

As on p. 144
① Apply adhesive to each of the
   tips of paper, and attach them
   to the main part of the basket.
② Stick the tips down one at a
   time. Then attach the handles.

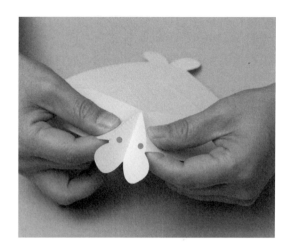

Make mountain folds, apply adhesive to the gray areas, then stick them together.

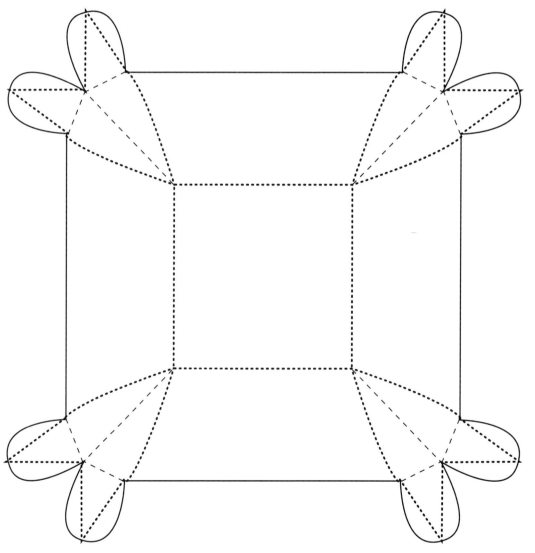

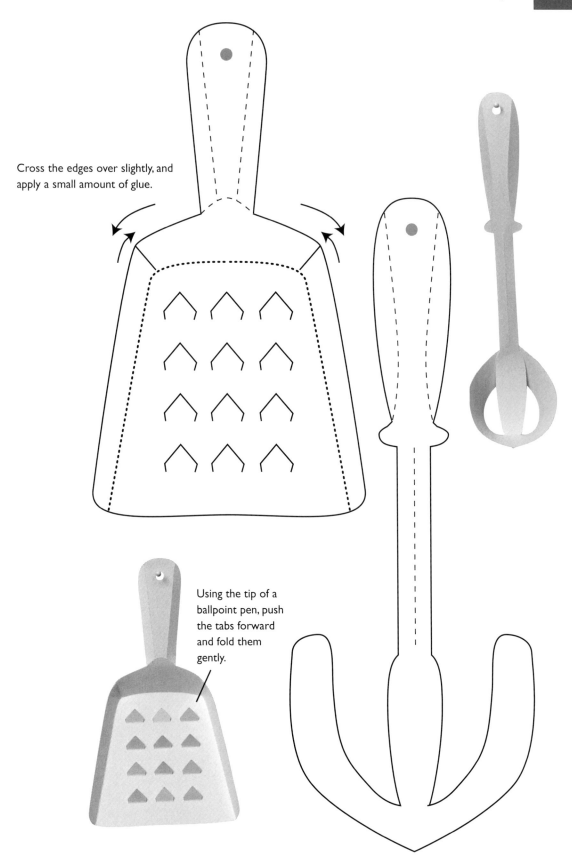

Cross the edges over slightly, and apply a small amount of glue.

Using the tip of a ballpoint pen, push the tabs forward and fold them gently.

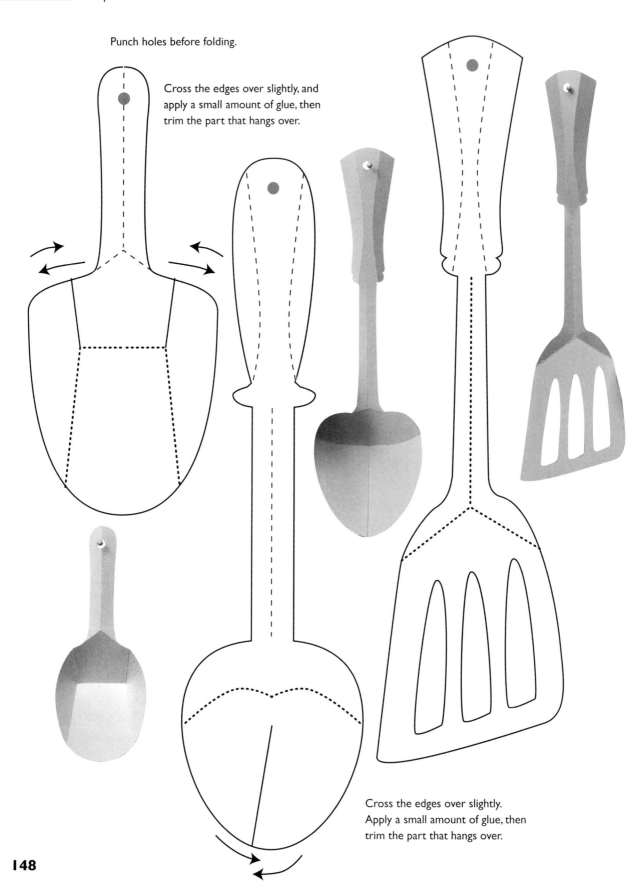

Punch holes before folding.

Cross the edges over slightly, and apply a small amount of glue, then trim the part that hangs over.

Cross the edges over slightly. Apply a small amount of glue, then trim the part that hangs over.

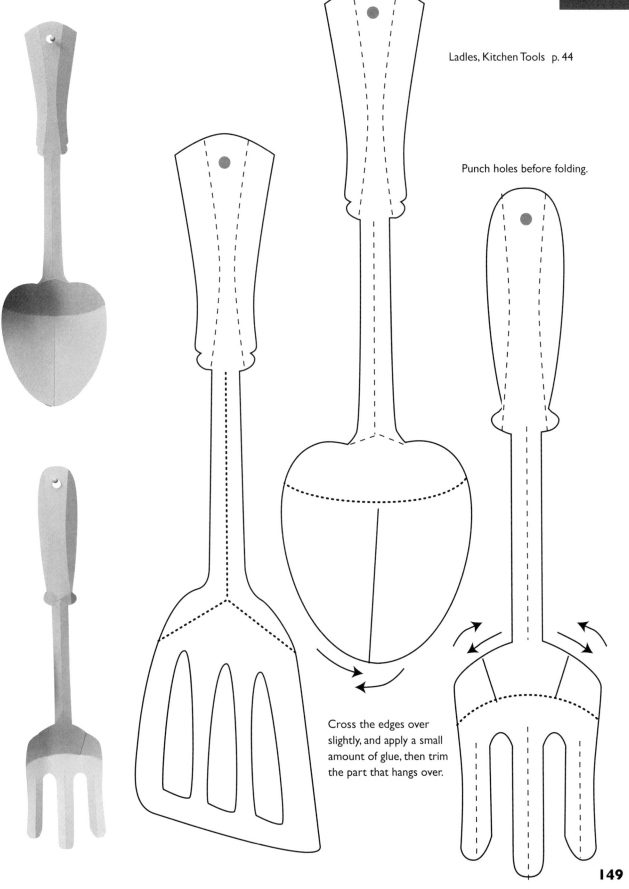

Ladles, Kitchen Tools p. 44

Punch holes before folding.

Cross the edges over
slightly, and apply a small
amount of glue, then trim
the part that hangs over.

How to Make 3-D Paper Chains

1 Check which direction the paper naturally bends.

Cut two thin strips (A and B), each measuring 3/4" (2 cm) x 5 7/8" (15 cm). One strip should be cut out of the drawing paper horizontally and the other vertically.

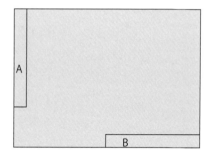

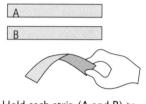

Hold each strip (A and B) to see which one bends more easily. Line up the letters and the pattern in the same direction as that strip.

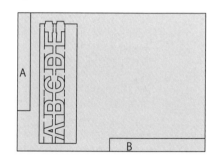

For example, if A bends more easily, line up the letters and pattern like this.

2 Line up the letters and the pattern.

Cut out a copy of each letter's pattern, and arrange the letters horizontally on a different piece of paper. Note: For letters in a chain, the patterns are not inverted.

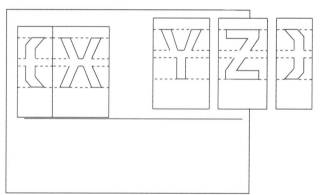

Enlarge a copy of the pasted letters, and use that as your pattern.

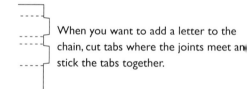

When you want to add a letter to the chain, cut tabs where the joints meet and stick the tabs together.

3 Make creases and cut out.

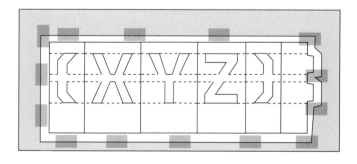

As with the other designs, fold the creased lines and cut the lines inside the design first. Then cut out the letters and patterns. Use a ruler when making creases with a ballpoint pen.

4 Fold the paper.

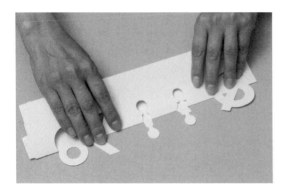

Always fold the letters and patterns on a desk or other flat surface, making sure not to go over the crease lines. Fold each crease sharply.

5 Apply adhesive, and stick the tabs together.

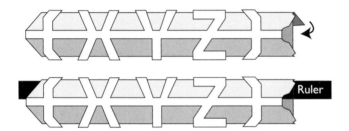

After putting the chain together loosely, dot a small amount of adhesive to the end tab, and fold it around a ruler or other straight edge. Press firmly.

6 Assemble the chain at the joints.

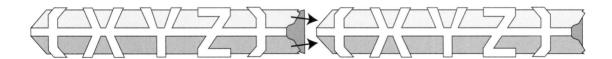

Link the chain together at the joints, and stick the chain on the wall.

Decorative Borders p. 45

Be sure to add a little bit extra length on each side. Leave 7/8" (2 cm) to 1 1/8" (3 cm) extra beyond the flower pattern on both the left and right ends to make it easier to connect the sections of the border.

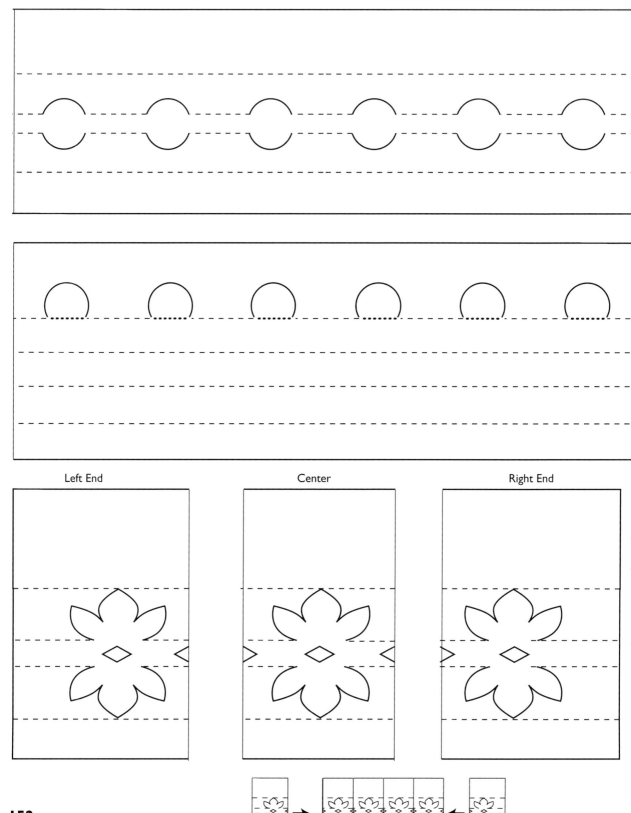

| Left End | Center | Right End |

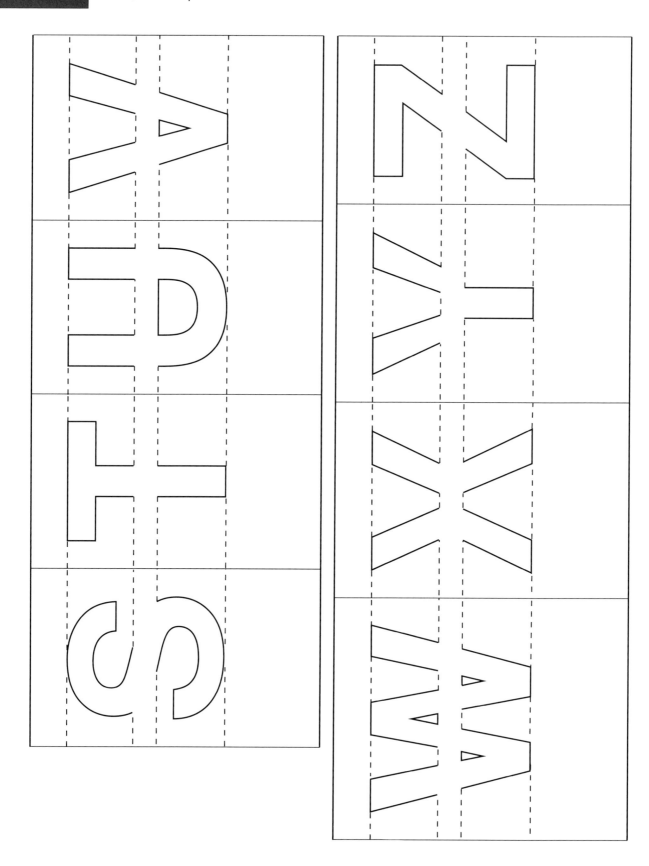

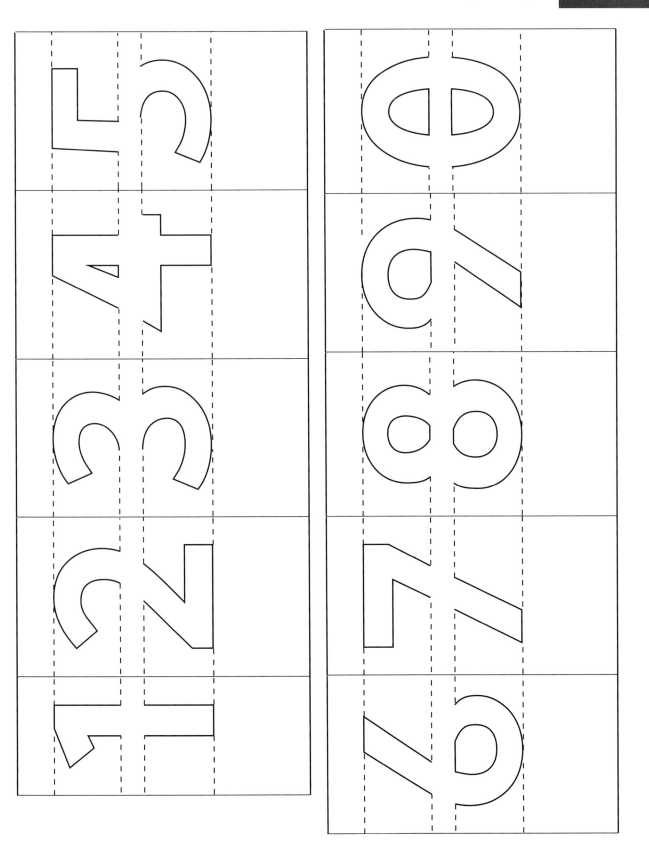

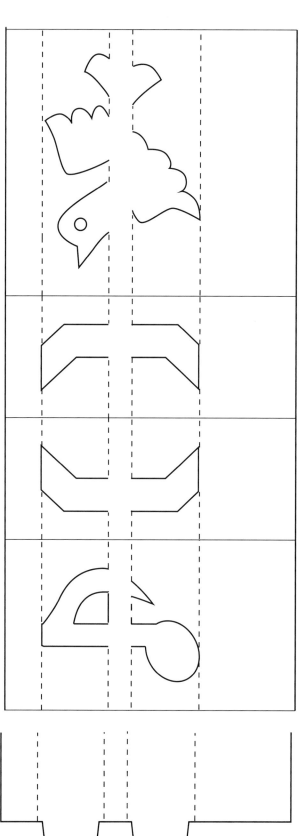

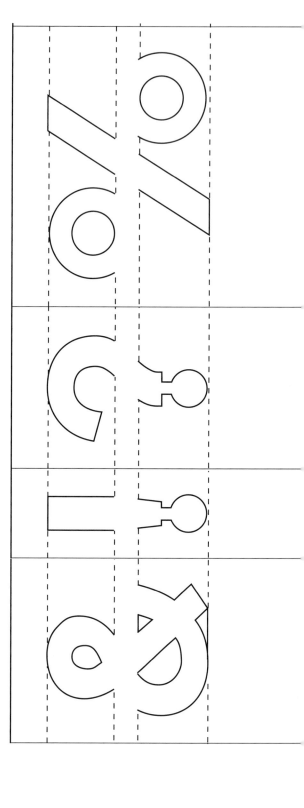

150%

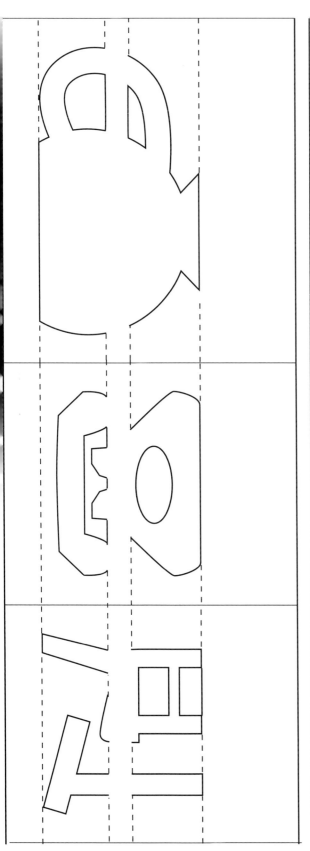

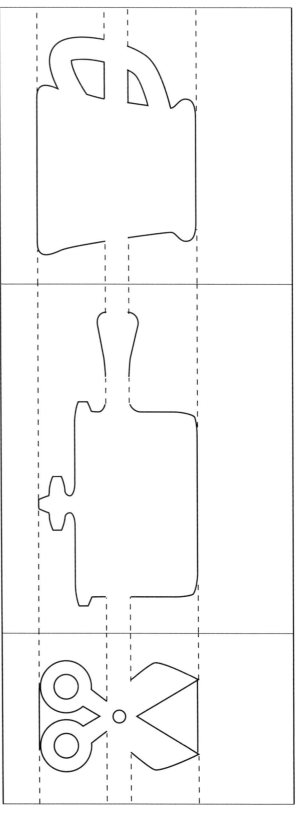